DEEPLY FLOW THE *Love* CURRENTS

~ A Love Story ~

Noel Francisco

www.trafford.com
North America & international
toll-free: 1 888 232 4444 (USA & Canada)
fax: 812 355 4082

A Love Story shared with seven vibrant granddaughters,* irreplaceable family members, cherished friends, and curious readers.

*D*edicated to Barbara, our granddaughters, and all who find their marriages or seek marriages that continually evolve into transforming experiences that excel one's fondest expectations!

(*What, no grandsons? No, no grandsons. So what?!)

Acknowledgements

$\mathcal{N}$ikkee Francisco, my granddaughter; Mollee Heinle, my granddaughter; and Denny Stanton, my son-in-law, provided invaluable assistance with their computer skills in the submission of this manuscript to Trafford Publishers.

Compared with these individuals, my computer skills are in the prekindergarten stage

Could a major factor be a generational one?

Contents

Part I
"I Think This Is It!"

Part II
New Territory

Part III
"Prof" and Family Life

Part IV
Life on the Changing Stage

Part V
Life Is, Indeed, Adventurous

Appendix

Foreword

*A*s usual, we were waiting on my grandparents.

It was karaoke night at the cabin and my cousins and I had the music queued up and were eager to get started. Every few minutes, we glanced out the window to see if they had yet emerged from the wooded path connecting the two homes. Each time, we were greeted with the same grandparent-less scene.

And then suddenly there they were, walking in the door, nearly unrecognizable, in the most absurd outfits you'd ever seen—short shorts and knee-high gym socks, my grandpa donning a neon orange hat, my grandma's short gray hair pulled into pigtails. We dissolved into fits of laughter.

None of us could imagine what had prompted their wardrobe selections that evening until it came time for their performance. Grandma and grandpa began to sing "Hello Muddah, Hello Faddah"— that novelty tune from the 1960s about a miserable little camper. They were off-key and off-beat, but we didn't care. A more perfect duo, we had never seen.

I'm not sure I can write about grandpa without writing about grandma. After more than 60 years of marriage, their lives were so intertwined that few would have been surprised if they journeyed on to heaven together, too. That didn't happen. My grandma passed away in 2011 and grandpa was forced to start the next chapter without her.

Several years before my grandma passed away, I suggested that grandpa write this book. I had been witness to much of the last three decades of their love story, sure, but I wanted to know the *whole* story.

I can still remember the beautiful summer evening when I asked grandma how she and grandpa first met. She told me a story about a handsome young man that drove her home from a church function one night. He had a girlfriend, but grandma's impish twinkle had caught his eye.

I couldn't wait to tell my sister and cousins about this stunning bit of news. Grandpa had a girlfriend before grandma! Silly as it may seem, it had never crossed my mind that my grandparents may have had other love interests—other lives even—before they met one another. In my mind, it had just always been Noel and Barbara.

In my mind, it always will be. This is their story.

-Mollee Francisco-Heinle

Noel and Barbara
1975

PART I

"I Think This Is It!"

Without love, humans long ago would have vanished.

Introduction

$\mathcal{N}$umerous individuals have exclaimed how our marriage was quite exceptional and unusual and have encouraged that I write a story about it. Several younger couples have also remarked how we in our marriage have been mentors for them. Until these thoughts had been expressed, I never considered about being mentors to others, or I likely would have been self—conscious about being around these people. As it is, this story is one of an ever—evolving marital relationship that seemed to come naturally and spontaneously. We knew our marital ties with one another were extremely meaningful and inspiring from early on and that each year our love for one another kept growing, but until the last few years, we never thought of our marital lives as being anything out of the ordinary. Apparently, when our marriage and love is compared with others as reported in the media, in studies, and social research, it has been rather noteworthy. As the following story develops, the reader can decide for herself/himself, whether or not this may be true.

Even if I had the vocabulary of classic writers, poets, and narrators, words would still prove most inadequate to describe Barbara's and my marriage. So, from the very beginning, this effort to describe it and share it, is a frustrating one. Oh, if that somehow one could capture in some tangible manner the real situations, the actual happenings, the love shared, and the enchantment of the days, months, and years our marriage evolved, how wonderful this would be. Falling far short of this, nevertheless, this writing is an effort to capture in word something of what, for Barbara and me, have been experiences that propel me to write about and share with you—our granddaughters, family, friends, and readers—the creative dynamics of our marriage. Even before we were married, we often repeated a thought that came to our minds as we were preparing for what lay ahead for us, namely, "life is adventurous." This we reminded ourselves of frequently during our sixty-two years of marriage, and truly, these years proved to be adventurous in their own special way. So we begin!

I Meet Her

*L*ittle did I realize what was down the pike when I finally met the little blonde nurse that my good friend, Dick Anthens, associate minister of Central Christian Church in downtown Des Moines, had been wanting me to meet. That the beginning of a marvelous marriage that would last for over sixty-two years was in the making, was beyond the range of my imagination. Although a few weeks later, after we had several dates, I did for the first time ever (and never wrote such again) write in my pocket appointment book, "I think this is it!" But this is getting ahead of the story.

I had been dating rather regularly an attractive girl who also attended Central Christian Church. Both she and Barbara were attending an evening religious education class at the church taught by Reverend Thens. Our dating in recent weeks had not been going very smoothly, so arrangements were made for me to drive them both home after their class. This I did, but I let Jan* out first at her home and then drove Barbara on the remaining couple of miles to her home. Of course, what I had in mind was the old strategy that this rather obvious maneuver would create some jealousy in Jan. But, the incident did create some unexpected interest on my part in Barbara. This little, blonde nurse did have a quiet, unassuming, poised personality that definitely got my attention. I decided, hoping that Barbara would feel the same way, that I would like to have the opportunity to learn to know her better. Whether or not I suggested a date later on, I do not recall for sure, but I know I wanted to have some reason (or excuse) to see her again in the near future. My interest in Jan was not jettisoned, but it was definitely made secondary, and my thoughts were focused on Barbara.

The opportunity came a few days later. Dick Anthens, who did not own a car, was planning to go up to Carrol, Iowa, where his wife had been visiting her parents who lived there. I offered to drive him there, and I asked Barbara if she would like to accompany us. She agreed, so to Carrol the three of us went. It was about a two—hour drive and provided unhurried opportunity for the three of us to visit. Dick helped to cover more introductory information (in an inconspicuous manner) about both of us as we drove to Carrol. After leaving Dick at his in-laws', we had the trip back to elaborate on the conversations we had had. We learned more about each other's thoughts, values, interests, etc. Our perspectives, likes, and dislikes, seemed to blend quite well, and by the time we returned to her home, we both knew we wanted to see more of each other.

One of the next dates was taking more chances than I realized at the time. We drove out to a town, only a short distance west of Des Moines, where a good friend of mine was the student minister at the church there. He and his wife had invited a number of us ministerial students, their wives, and girl friends to their home for a fun night of games and refreshments. We played a card game (hearts or something like that) where you could gang up on a player and load him down with losing cards. We all knew (except Barbara) one another quite well and were unrestrained in our kidding of each other. Well, they ganged up on me, which they liked to do, and the evening was a noisy, loud, and wild one, with me often the target of their teasing.

Barbara was not accustomed to such reverie, but she took it all in good stride. She was not deterred from consenting to meet each other for lunch in downtown Des Moines in the next few days.

We both worked in downtown Des Moines. She was the office nurse for a prominent doctor there, and I worked as a probation officer for the Polk County Juvenile Court with offices in the county courthouse, only a few blocks away from her physician's office building. So, it was quite convenient for us to meet and have lunch together. It was after one of these luncheon dates, that I wrote in my appointment book, "I think this is it!"

We had some evening dates also at this time, and on one of these dates, I remember the subject of our ages was mentioned. Now, I guess that Barbara, in some way, knew that Jan was several years older than I (in fact, I had found out several months earlier that Jan was six years older than I, which at first tended to throw me for a "loop"!) So as Barbara and I explicitly shared with each other our ages and it came out that Barbara was eleven months older than I, I well remember that she immediately exclaimed, "Oh, that's not enough to make any difference!" Our age difference never did have any effect upon our relationship. Later on in our marriage, I would teasingly say that she needed to recall that I was younger than she was, so she should give me special care. The dates continued rather frequently, and a growing, meaningful friendship and companionship grew. There was nothing frivolously romantic, in the popular sense, about those days. We just thoroughly enjoyed each other's company. We often double-dated, especially with Anita and Court Adams. I had known Court early on in fourth grade in Ft. Madison, Iowa, and our families had kept in touch with one another ever since then. (They soon moved to New York state from Ft. Madison, and through correspondence and occasional meetings at church conventions, the families continued their friendship.) When I came out to finish my undergraduate work and engage in graduate work at Drake University, I roomed for a short time with Court, who was already attending Drake. When he married Anita, they lived for a short time in my apartment while I was gone for part of the summer. They soon rented a small apartment in the next block, and Barbara and I were often guests at their place. We also packed picnic lunches and went with them on picnics to various parks in Des Moines, where the four of us greatly enjoyed the fellowship we experienced. Anita soon obtained, with her business background, the position of being secretary to the dean of the seminary, where she was well situated to keep track of us ministerial students. She did not like it when I occasionally would have a date with anyone other than Barbara.

This "lifestyle" continued for about a year. Barbara and I had no explicit commitment to each other, but we knew we both thought a great deal of each other. When I began to realize that our relationship was becoming definitely serious, I thought I had better, at least temporarily, slow down the affair. There was a girl back in Illinois that I guess was sort of my "dream girl," and I thought I had better find out what the potential was for any relationship with her. Of course, I told Barbara about this, and for a period of time, we sort of signed off while I looked into the matter of this person back in Illinois. It was not a decision that she cared about, and I had my reservations about the matter too, but in all fairness, I believed I should clear up the situation before Barbara and I became any more serious with each other. Consequently, there was an interruption in our dating and courtship that went on for several months.

A Commitment Is Made

he inquiry into the "dream girl" back in Illinois did not indicate any likely developing courtship with her. I saw her once when I was back in Illinois and talked about our possible dating, and I phoned her from Des Moines a few times, but I knew she really was not interested in dating me. So, I dropped the matter and settled back to a more or less dateless life in Des Moines. For some reason, I did not contact Barbara during this period. I don't recall any specific reason for this other than maybe I sort of wanted to think things through.

Then one evening, my phone rang in my room, and it was Barbara. She wanted to know if I would come over and that she wanted to talk with me. Without hesitation, I said I would come over. I understand that when her parents were told that I was driving over to their place, they quickly cleared the premises so that we could be alone while we talked. Barbara's father was strongly in favor of encouraging our relationship and was persistent and cooperative in this regard throughout our dating. I liked her parents and soon learned to feel at ease in their presence. But this one night might have been an exception!

We soon became engaged in serious conversation, and after she learned that the Illinois girl was out of the picture, she wondered why we couldn't resume dating. I certainly was not hostile to the idea, but I was hesitant about becoming seriously involved at that time. I asserted that our dating would be on a "platonic level" (famous last words!) and that I wished not to become involved beyond that level. She agreed (I think somewhat reluctantly) to this arrangement, and so we commenced dating again as good friends. In retrospect, I think I was not fully in accord with my sort of terms of what our relationship would be!

Very soon, our dating picked up the routine,—if one can refer to it as a routine—, where we had left off several months earlier. We often met downtown for lunch together, took in a movie from time to time, saw Anita and Court at their apartment where we often played cards went on picnics with them and other couples, and now and then went to various places with Barbara's parents, such as leisurely strolls through the beautiful Des Moines lilac gardens. Barbara also frequently accompanied me to Zearing, where I was the student minister. She stayed on Saturday nights at the Herr home, where arrangements had been made by the church for me to stay on weekends. She was soon "adopted" by the Herrs, and a strong friendship with them formed, which would last in a most meaningful way throughout the rest of their lives and their children's lives. Their home became a home away from home. Of course, Lou Herr, who liked to tease, often kidded Barbara and me, and this added to the camaraderie we enjoyed with them. Gradually and steadily, and more or less unbeknown to me, our relationship was taking on a steady and more profound character. We enjoyed each other's company, felt at ease with each other, sensed no need to conceal our thoughts from each other, and made no effort to avoid the deepening friendship that was developing. The "platonic nature" of the dating process was fast fading from the picture. We were more and more in love with one another, but we never explicitly discussed this fact. It was not the Hollywood or popular romantic novels version we were experiencing—a love that others might dub less spectacular and sensational, but a love that was growing quietly in the depths of our beings.

As we did become more aware of what was happening, I recall taking a walk one evening out in Barbara's neighborhood, and I pointed out that I hoped our love would not be the couple—centered type that emphasized a desire to be alone and "build a sweet, little nest and let the rest of the world go by" as the lines to a classic old love song read. Rather, as I gestured, let it be a love that embodied a closeness with each other but was pointed outward, which I characterized by holding my two index fingers together with the fingers pointing out from us. This symbolism is what we used from time to time through the rest of our dating and during our marriage. In our growing love, we wished to remember the larger world beyond us with its many problems, pains, and joys.

In the spring of 1948, we went to a dance at one of the popular dance halls in the Des Moines area. A big—time dance band, Les Brown and his renowned band I believe was the featured orchestra. It was a beautiful, mild spring evening, and when we came back to her home and were sitting in my car in her folks' driveway, I asked her if she would marry me. Without hesitation, she said she would (I would really have been thrown for a spin if she had answered negatively!), and we became formally engaged. I gave her my Lambda Chi fraternity pin, which was customary for many fraternity men to seal symbolically an engagement. It was a romantic evening in many ways, but we did not magnify the event to each other or to our friends. It was a good feeling, and our sense of well—being with each other was further deepened.

It Almost Didn't Happen!

*M*uch of the summer of 1948 was spent in completing some odds and ends at Drake, such as handing in my Master's thesis. Some time that summer, Barbara went back to Pekin with me to meet friends there and visit in my parents' home. Of course, she had met my parents on several of their visits to Des Moines. Dorothy Jenks, a long time friend of our family, also had a bridal shower for Barbara. I was glad for Barbara to have the opportunity to visit the environment in which I grew up.

Back in Des Moines, we set the date, August 18th, for our wedding. My father and the minister at Barbara's home church in Des Moines, Rev. Ben Bobbit of Central Christian Church, would participate in the wedding. Then I planned a trip up north with my parents, which, as it turned out, could have shut the door of our wedding! Just a couple of weeks before the wedding, my parents and I drove to a small resort near Danbury, Wisconsin.

I thought a break from all the rather frenzied activities in Des Moines could be relaxing and calming. I remember that a picnic lunch had been brought along on our drive up to Wisconsin, and when we stopped at a roadside park for lunch, that being just with my father and mother at this picturesque park was a memorable experience. The week at this Wisconsin resort was peaceful and enjoyable until I began to work on writing our wedding ceremony. I had volunteered myself (with Barbara's approval!) to write this. As I sat out in front of our cabin writing the ceremony, I began to think about the commitment this was entailing, and I had some mild reservations begin to form, which became more pronounced as I continued to work on the ceremony. Was I really ready to make this profound commitment? Just what was down the pike for us? Was I emotionally mature enough to enter into marriage? In those days, the thought that the marriage could be terminated by divorce, never was considered as a realistic option. There were no doubts about Barbara; the doubts were about myself.

By the end of the week's vacation, I had worked myself into a state of considerable anxiety.

I had written Barbara about the uncertainities that were developing in my mind about the wedding and had stated that I thought we had better plan to have some talks about them and that I would return to Des Moines a couple of days sooner than I had planned. My former landlord offered to let me stay in my old room, rent free, while back for our wedding. I drove out to the Youngses soon after getting settled in my room, and Barbara and I drove out to the edge of Des Moines to a scenic overlook of the surrounding countryside, and there we began to talk. I shared with her my misgivings about whether or not I was ready to make the commitment that I believed marriage entailed, and she listened understandingly. She also shared with me her feelings about some anxiety on her part about the situation. We had a searching, open, and frank talk about it all. Neither of us wanted then flatly to call off the wedding. We knew we had deep, affectionate feelings toward each other, and we did not want to end them. After a somewhat lengthy conversation, we decided, somewhat tentatively, to go ahead with the wedding. The prospects of the wedding being a touch—and—go matter were rather emotionally draining for us. Certainly, we both felt the tension that was present in our considerations. There was no arguing nor unpleasantedness in our attitudes expressed toward each other—just free, honest sharing of how we felt about being married.

Someone should have told us that experiences such as the ones we were having were common with couples on the eve of their weddings, but we accepted the fact that what was happening to us was a serious development and that we needed to face and confront forthrightly our reservations. For us, it was a tense and critical few hours. Never again, though, during the many years of our marriage, did I ever have any doubts or misgivings about our having been married. As Frank Gardner used to say about his decision to marry Helen, his wife, it was the best decision he ever made. I felt this, too, in the decision to marry Barbara, and those uncertain feelings and thoughts a few days before August 18th never again reoccurred or even came close to reoccurring!

That night, I slept well, and Barbara told me later that she did too. She later told me that if she had awakened that morning with the misgivings she had felt the night before when we talked, that she would not have gone ahead with the wedding. That morning, I felt a relieved peace of mind that I had not experienced for several days. I had no hesitation about the wedding and looked forward to the small informal, wedding we had planned. At the last moment, we had changed our plans, and instead of having it in the chapel of her church, we had decided to have an outdoor ceremony. I felt that an outdoor wedding on a beautiful summer morning would be more conducive to the relaxed, tension-free moments we wished for this occasion. The chapel also had furnishings that Barbara's family had given to the church in memory of her mother, who had been killed in a car accident several years earlier. These furnishings could have been some detraction from the actual wedding, and an outside wedding could avoid this. We had asked Judge Meyers and Mrs. Meyers if we could have the wedding in their spacious yard with its beautiful flower beds, and they willingly consented. Judge Meyers had been the juvenile court judge under whom I worked as a probation officer, and he and his family were close friends of Dick and Edith Anthens who were attending the wedding. In fact, Dick was the best man at our wedding. It was a small wedding party with Idris Vernon (Scott) serving as Barbara's bridesmaid. Only our parents (Bertha, Barbara's stepmother, who was fully accepted by all of us), and some family members and Judge and Mrs. Meyers were present.

The ceremony went smoothly. Dick Anthens, on our way down the yard to stand before my father and Reverend Bobbit, waved a little flag at me, reminiscent of us being color guards together at our Drake commencement march earlier that spring, when he lowered the flag for me to catch as rehearsed as we passed through the door into the auditorium and he proceeded to knock off my mortar cap in front of the governor of Iowa and other dignitaries. This humor helped to moderate any exaggerated solemnity to the occasion. One clause in the ceremony that I wrote and that I later said I regretted omitting, was the traditional phrase in wedding ceremonies when the bride makes the pledge to "love and obey" her husband. What an oversight on my part! (I can just see Barbara seriously making such a pledge!)

After the wedding, we all drove to downtown Des Moines where Barbara's parents had made arrangements for a private, informal wedding luncheon at the Grace Ransom Tea Room—one of Des Moines' restaurants noted for its gourmet food. The camaraderie was quite spontaneous and pleasant. The luncheon seemed to be a quite appropriate conclusion to the wedding activities in Des Moines.

The Wedding Trip

We left for our wedding trip soon after the dinner at Grace Ransom Tea Room. I had planned ahead of time to have reservations for where we would stay on our trip to northern Minnesota and attempted to follow suggestions for the trip, which had been noted in the family course I had had in a sociology class at Drake. In fact, for me, I thought I had been rather systematic and thorough in the plans I made.

The first "hitch" in these plans came a few days before the trip when I received a communication from the motel where I had made reservations for the first night that my reservation had been canceled. I forgot the exact reason for the cancellation, but I believe it had to do with something about being overbooked for the night of my reservation. But this did not concern us, especially since we would be going through the Twin Cities, and surely, we would have no difficulty in renting a room in a hotel or motel in such a large metropolitan area. But this was not to be. When we arrived in Minneapolis and planned to check in to one of the larger hotels there, we were informed they had no vacancies and that nearly every facility in the Twin Cities was booked solidly for a rural mailmen's convention that was being held. We were told that we might have a better chance of finding accommodations in St. Paul. So hurriedly we drove to St. Paul.

We chose to inquire at an older hotel where we might have a better chance of finding a room. So we chose the Hotel Ryan in downtown St. Paul. Fortunately, they had one vacancy—the salesman room. Most of the room was an empty, one except for stored tables where salesmen could spread out their sample goods for potential customers to view. There was a small sort of alcove that had a bed in it. We took the room.

Now the Hotel Ryan had been a Victorian structure that probably was one of the pride and joys of St. Paul several generations earlier, but its glory days were in the past. Our room was on the second floor, and we parked our car on the street, below the window of our room.

Practically all my worldly possessions were packed in our car. The story that was embellished upon every time that Frank Gardner told it (and he did enjoy telling it) was that I was up at least every hour, looking out the window to be sure our car was not being broken in to. This account was only partially true. I am not sure the hotel had a parking garage, but since we were trying to be extra careful to conserve our limited funds, we parked the car on the street. Fortunately, considering the part of downtown St. Paul where we stayed, the car was spared a break-in.

The next morning, we resumed our trip to Seni Omsed Resort (Des Moines spelled backwards) on Woman Lake. Back a couple of weeks earlier, I had inquired from some of the people I knew in Des Moines if they were aware of any resort in northern Minnesota that had modern facilities. (Modern facilities back in the 1940s were not too common in resorts in Minnesota.) One of these persons had been to Seni Omsed and recommended it. So I had made reservations there. We arrived there in the early afternoon and were escorted to the cabin which had been reserved for us. It was named "Wee Inn," and it was small. It was modern, though. It had a closet-like bathroom in it with only a toilet—qualifying for it to be considered modern!

I was hoping that we would appear as a couple who had been married for some time. I was concerned, though, that I would introduce Barbara as my wife, Miss Youngs, since for over two years, I had been so introducing her as such. (Back then, for brides to retain their maiden name was very unusual.) But I avoided this error. I thought we were doing well in passing as a couple who were not newlyweds. But as we were getting settled in "Wee Inn," I noticed the camp boy, a lad in his late teens, was standing by the front screen door, staring in on us. Apparently, we had not fooled him!

The resort did have beautiful, spacious grounds, and in spite of its spartan accommodations, it was a pleasant place to be. Wee Inn had a screened—in porch in addition to the larger single room that contained the kitchen and sort of a living room/bedroom arrangement. We liked sleeping in the bed on the screened-in porch. But one night, it rained quite intensely, and there was a quite noticeable steady leak over the side of the bed in which Barbara was sleeping. She did not especially care for this wet lullaby she was receiving, but sleepily, I did not give the situation much attention. Then the leaks spread, and I began to get wet from a leak over my side of the bed. We moved inside. The cabin should have been called "Wee-leaky-inn"—(or maybe not, in view of the connotation today with that term!).

One day, we went fishing over at a small lake where a couple of summers earlier I had been successful in catching fish. This was one of the few times that Barbara went fishing with me. She enjoyed fishing, but for some unknown reason, she did not show interest in the sport in ensuing years. We had good luck in fishing and brought back to our cabin a good mess for our evening meal. I cleaned the fish and left them in the kitchen sink for Barbara to fry and stepped outside to visit with our next—door neighbors. The visit continued longer than I had anticipated, and still Barbara did not call to say that supper was ready. Finally, I went inside only to find Barbara sitting down, reading a book, and the fish were still in the sink where I had left them. She said, when I looked puzzled, that she did not know how to fry fish. What a blow this was! (Kidding, of course.) So I fried the fish, and we had our supper around midnight that night.

Of course, the few days we were at Seni—Omsed were memorable days, and the simple facilities, but beautiful surroundings only added to the romantic memories our stay there had for us. This wedding trip was Barbara's first visit to the North Country. I wanted her to like this forested lake country, for I had numerous, fond boyhood memories of vacations in this area, and I hoped she would begin to have the same. On our way back to Des Moines, we drove down a different highway from Woman Lake to Pine River, and unbeknown to us at the time, we passed within one-half mile of the lake property that we would be purchasing eight years later. Northwoods sand was getting in our shoes in proportions far beyond what we would have imagined back then.

When we arrived back at Barbara's parents in Des Moines, we had already spent a major portion of what I had saved for going out to Duke. Earlier that summer, I had sold my pride and joy, a rather classy car, and purchased an older car from my landlord in Des Moines, which provided about five hundred extra dollars to start our Duke days. In spite of some efforts to be frugal, something had happened to most of that five hundred dollars! It looked like we had some belt-tightening days ahead!

PART II

New Territory

Since prehistoric times, humans have been on the move.

We Arrive in Durham and Duke

efore driving on to Durham, we stopped at my parents' home in Pekin and visited there a couple of days. We also stopped to see my grandmothers in Findlay, Illinois. They were anxious to meet Barbara. Later, I found out that my grandmother Melcher had made plans to come out to Des Moines with my parents and be present at our wedding. In the hurried and uncertain preparations for proceeding with the wedding, she was forgotten. I hated this very much, and still when I think about it, I am upset by my thoughtlessness. Nevertheless, we had a brief, but creative and inspiring visit with my grandmothers.

We arrived in Durham with no idea where we would be staying. I had attempted to line up a small apartment, but the arrangements, for some reason I forget now, were unable to be finalized for this renting. Duke back then had very limited housing for married students. We were able to obtain a reference at one of the Duke offices for a room in a private home where we stayed the first couple of nights. Then we found another home where we could rent a bedroom with cooking privileges in the kitchen. This was in a rather higher—income residential area of Durham, and the aristocratic widow lady who had the home was very gracious and accommodating. We stayed with her for a couple of weeks, and then located in a different part of Durham, a small duplex which we rented. As was the case with numerous lower-income houses, this duplex was built on short pillars with no other foundation. The wind on colder days had free circulation under the building. Our part of the duplex consisted of a larger combination bedroom/living room, a small kitchen, and a screened—in hallway, which led to the bathroom at the back of the house, which we shared with the couple who lived in the other part of the duplex. The couple who occupied the other side soon became our good friends. He was a law student at Duke, and they, too, were newlyweds.

Our furnishings were spartan, but satisfactory. Our refrigerator sat just outside the kitchen door in the screened—in hallway that led to the bathroom. We found out that there were large cockroaches in that part of the house, so we put blocks under the legs of the refrigerator and scattered fluoride powder around the blocks to prevent the roaches from getting in the refrigerator. We were contented with our accommodations; however, as cold weather began to develop, we found our apartment was a rather drafty place. The heating stove we had was a wood—burning one and did not heat parts of the apartment that were farther removed from it.

There was a somewhat older graduate student in the department who was rather uninhibited in what she said. She called us men "precious," and this did not go down too well with us. We tried to avoid meeting her in the main library for she was, as likely as not, to say quite audibly in the quiet environment of the library, "Oh, precious," as she greeted us. She found out about our plight with our old-fashioned heating stove and went to the Dean of the Graduate School and told him there were graduate students, naming our names, who were living in health-threatening conditions where we were nearly freezing on cold mornings! I was fearful of being called in to the Dean's office to describe our living conditions, but nothing so far as I knew ever resulted from her report on our living situation. This, also, was about as close as I ever got to the Graduate Dean's office during all my residency at Duke!

Within a couple of weeks, Barbara was given a job at the large municipal hospital in Durham. She was put in charge of a large polio ward without scarcely any preparation for the assignment. There was a polio epidemic that Fall, and hospitals were badly in need of nurses for the polio patients. During the few days she was at this hospital, there was a small, electrical fire in the polio ward, and Barbara immediately reported it to the main office. But nothing happened, and finally, she called back and said, "Say we had a fire down here, which I reported, and there was no response to this emergency call." Someone did come then to check on the matter, but by then, the fire had been extinguished. These few days were enough for Barbara at this medical facility, and when she was called about an opening as day-time nurse in the Duke Women's Infirmary, she gladly accepted the position. She continued through the school year, working in the infirmary, and without any complaints, gladly set her mind to earning her HPHTS degree (spelled out—Help Poor Hubby Through School!)

It was an exciting year for us. This was a new country for us, and when we could, we enjoyed driving out through the red clay—covered countryside and seeing the numerous small tobacco farms. We drove over one weekend to the coast and stayed one night in an old southern tourist home. The next morning, we awakened to snow on the ground! This was not what we had come to North Carolina to see! Nevertheless, we enjoyed seeing the Atlantic Ocean for the first time, and traveling there was a favorite past time in the ensuing years.

The Graduate Sociology Department at Duke was not a large department, and numerous friendships developed, which we valued very much. Some of the professors had us on a few occasions in their home for a social evening. These events were always much appreciated. Without knowing it at the time, these informal (and even more formal) experiences were weaving an even stronger bond between Barbara and me. In today's vernacular, we were "bonding" more and more. It was thrilling to be sharing and experiencing what we did in a new and exciting environment. Duke and Durham were a good place to be!

Winding Up the First Year
at Duke and Durham

$\mathcal{W}$e liked living in the small duplex and stayed there for several months. We enjoyed the friendship with Wade and Libby,— the law student and his wife who occupied the other side of the duplex, and we were glad to be helping out the landlady who lived next door by renting her duplex. She and her husband were working—class people with several small children, and we were sure that they lived "hand-to-mouth." Barbara and Libby worked with her in an attempt to show her how she could buy more wisely, and she seemed to appreciate their good intentions. Barbara and I enjoyed hearing her small children play outside and talk with a noticeable (at least to us) southern accent.

We did go back to Iowa for our first Christmas together. We took a route in West Virginia that wound around through the edge of the mountains as we approached Charleston. Later, when we saw the winding, narrow road that we had traveled that December night, we were rather shocked that we had driven on such a treacherous—appearing road. We stayed in a tourist home in Charleston, West Virginia, that first night and it had a gas heater in the bedroom, and the glow and flames of this heater, warmed our souls as well as our bodies.

My parents had moved to Centerville, Iowa, where my father had accepted the pastorate of the Christian Church—one of the larger churches in this small, southern Iowa city. It was an old, very comfortable parsonage with very thick walls and a special charm of its own. We enjoyed the week we spent with my parents that first Christmas, and to add to the joy of being there, Barbara's parents drove down from Des Moines to be with all of us for Christmas. The ground was well covered with snow, and it was a picturesque Christmas we never forgot.

We drove back to Durham by a different route. On New Year's night, we were in the mountains of northwestern North Carolina when the generator on the old Dodge ceased functioning, and to conserve the battery, we coasted down some of the roads and made it to Winston-Salem. We were doubtful if we would be able to find a garage open on a holiday night where we might have the generator repaired. We luckily found a one—stall garage open, and the mechanic installed new brushes in the generator. When we finally got back to Durham, late that New Year's night, I had fifty cents left in my pocket!!

Our landlady tried to accommodate us as best she could on her limited income, and when we returned from our Christmas trip, we found that she had installed a new oil heating stove in our duplex, which we definitely appreciated. Yet, we sort of wished for a little larger and more modern apartment or duplex. In the early spring, we looked in the Sunday newspaper at apartments for rent, and one that was advertised sort of caught our eye. It was the upstairs of a private home in another section of Durham, which stated that it contained a front living room, another sitting room, a bedroom, kitchen, and bath. We did not seriously think we would change our place of residence, but out of curiosity, more than anything, we went and looked at it early on a Sunday morning. We liked the people who owned the home. The apartment, compared with the little duplex, was to us a palace, and the rent was what we could afford. We ended up renting it. We went from renting the apartment to the downtown Methodist church in Durham, and I fear I heard little, if any, of the church service that morning. My mind was on the apartment we had rented and how we could fix it up into a very desirable home. We were both very excited about the prospects of living in a pleasing apartment. We had thought we would be unable to cover the rent for such a nice apartment; it almost seemed as if we had stumbled in to a dream world.

While we hated to leave our little duplex and the landlady and her family, we were quite anxious to get settled in our new apartment. Wade and Libby, we soon found out, had rented a new modern duplex not far from where we were moving. We had not been long in our new apartment when Idris Vernon, Barbara's close friend and roommate in nurse's training, came to visit us. We were glad we had a roomy apartment to entertain a guest like Idris. Felix and Bessie Fuquay, who owned the house in which we were renting the upstairs apartment, were very congenial. And although we did not know it then, this was the beginning of one of our dear Durham friendships. We would enjoy numerous visits, outings, and varied events with them in months ahead. The bus went right by the Fuquay home, and Barbara found this convenience great for riding to the Women's Infirmary. The front room even had a small roll down top desk and made an ideal place for me to study. We couldn't have been any happier!

Certainly, we were never flushed with money and had to watch carefully our expenditures. One day in the mail arrived a letter from Centerville, Iowa. The letter was from a dentist in the church where Dad was the pastor, and enclosed in the letter was a check for one hundred dollars. We were totally surprised and could scarcely believe what we were seeing. If the check had had another zero attached to it, we couldn't have been any more elated. Later, we found out that this dentist had had a younger brother who had been away in college, studying to be a clergyman. The brother had become ill and died while attending college. The dentist told my parents that he knew what a struggle it was to finance one's way through college, and in memory of his brother, he was sending us this check. This unexpected happening relieved some of the pressures on our finances. The incident reminded us again of the many good people who inhabit our earth!

For the most part, I found my studies at Duke challenging and valuable. However, at times, I felt that some of my professors conveyed the impression that I had come from an inferior Midwest university with standards considerably below those of Duke. I naturally resented this. And one day, I stopped by Dr. Howard Jensen's office, the chairman of the Sociology Department, and in the course of our conversation, I told him how I felt about the way a prestigious eastern university looked down on the schools from which some of us Midwestern students had matriculated. I also stated that, much of the time, the faculty seemed rather remote from their students. Dr. Jensen had upset me earlier by marking up with red ink a paper I had handed him to read that I thought was one of my most creative writings. (The paper, incidentally was not a part of any classes I was taking from him or any other Duke faculty member. It was just a paper in which I had taken considerable pride, and I had handed it to him as a friendly gesture.) I could tell that my candid conversation angered him, and we had a rather prolonged review of the matter. (Later on, Dr. Jensen became a mentor for me and a cherished personal friend.) I guess I was a little offended at times by the fact that I did possess three university degrees (all from Drake), and yet I was treated at times, as if I were a rank freshman with little educational background.

Attitudes like this and other incidents that seemed to reflect an air of eastern superiority made me wonder if I wanted to continue my education at Duke the coming school year. Although, at the moment, our finances were not in any crucial state of affairs, the money to support another year at Duke seemed somewhat uncertain. Barbara and I did not worry especially about our plans for the forthcoming school year, but we did begin to explore what our options might be!

One possible option in the making was a vacancy in the position of superintendent in the joint city/county juvenile detention home. We contacted individuals who were responsible for filling this vacancy and expressed interest in the position. But nothing definite was done. The juvenile court judge who would be our immediate boss had indicated the salary would be two hundred and fifty dollars a month plus our board and room. Then when we indicated that we were quite serious in filling the vacancy, she quoted us a salary of two hundred dollars a month and board and room. We decided to hold out for the original quote she had given us.

At the end of the spring semester at Duke, we planned to go back to Iowa and stay for a short time with my parents in Centerville, Iowa. The juvenile detention home position was left open depending on whether or not the juvenile court judge and city and county officials would make the salary the original quote which had been given to us. They knew the address and phone number of my parents in Iowa where we could be reached.

We left a steamer trunk full of clothes and other possessions with the Fuquays, which we said we would pick up in case we came back to Durham and took the position at the juvenile detention home (referred to locally as the Youth Home), or otherwise, we would pay the shipping charges to have it shipped to us. While back in Iowa, I looked into the possibilities of transferring to the State University of Iowa in Iowa City. We hoped the offer from the people back in Durham would come through at the salary we were holding out for. Later on in June, the offer was made, and we accepted it and prepared to return to Durham during the latter part of June. We were glad to be returning to Durham and Duke, but we were not nearly as excited about it all as we had been a year earlier, when we were then moving in to new territory.

I would be the superintendent of the Home, and Barbara would be the matron. From the viewpoint of the hiring people back in Durham, I think they felt they were getting a "bargain"! They were hiring two professional people—one with experience in juvenile court work and the other a registered nurse—all for the salary of one! We were aware that we would be working twenty-four hours daily together, and the thought crossed our minds "Would such an arrangement be a strain on our relationship?" We were not too concerned with this possibility, for our first year of marriage had been a wonderful year for us, and our compatibility with one another was never in question. It would be a creative challenge for us!

Superintendent and Matron of the Durham Youth Home

The Durham Youth Home (juvenile detention home) was less than two years old. It was a T-shaped brick building with two rooms and a bath in each section of the cross T. A wall divided the sections to accommodate separate quarters for black and white males in one T and in the other T, the same for black and white females. It could house sixteen delinquents. At the front center of the T were our living quarters, consisting of bedroom and bath and a living room. Between our quarters and the detainees' sleeping quarters was a small guest room, and in the other direction was a bathroom off the main hallway. In the lower part of the stem of the T was a dining room, a kitchen, an office, and an examination room off the office. Below the kitchen and office were two "rumpus rooms" for indoor recreation. At the bottom of the stem, was a furnace room and coal room. A door between the kitchen and one of the rumpus rooms led out to a fenced—in playground. The fence around this playground was high, with strands of barbed wire across the top.

Near us, on the same government property, was the county tuberculosis sanatorium. We shared a large power mower for cutting the extensive grounds that surrounded the two institutions. On back behind us was a large field that covered several acres and went on up to the Durham County Home. All of this was government property. At the time we were at the Youth Home, there was little residential development in that part of Durham. (Since then, the city has spread out, and the open countryside has been invaded by residential developments.) There was, however, across the road from us, the main warehouses of Liggett and Meyer Tobacco Company. One could smell tobacco in the air much of the time—especially on warm summer days!

Such was the general physical environment where we would spend the next three and one-half years. It was rolling countryside and rather picturesque. We purchased some metal patio chairs and enjoyed, when we could, sitting out in front and viewing our surroundings. As our budget allowed, we did some landscaping to our immediate grounds and added, so we thought, to the pleasant appearance of the home. Included in our budget were the resources for hiring a cook and cleaning lady, and within two weeks, we had hired a middle-aged black lady, who stayed at the home all the time we were there. Gradually, she became a cherished friend and a definite asset to the home.

I guess I felt a little bit carried away with being superintendent of the home and after Alice, the cook and cleaning lady, had been with us for a couple of weeks, I made out a week's schedule of work assignments for Alice, to which she paid no attention! Of course, I made out no such schedule for Barbara, for I knew she would ignore it! The matter was dropped and not attempted again!

We would liked to have had a dog for us and the home and I mentioned this to Judge Walker, our immediate boss, but she ruled out the idea. She was afraid it might bite the children. I also had a tense session with Judge Walker in her downtown office over the time I was to put in at the home. I wanted to arrange for my classes at Duke for the forthcoming school year, and she practically negated any time for this, saying it would take me away for too long a period of time from the home. So, I proceeded to enumerate the number of hours we were putting in at the home by having to be available twenty-four hours a day and how when one looked at all these hours, what the classes at Duke consumed was barely noticeable. She dropped the subject, and it never came up again.

In numerous ways, we were finding out that working under Judge Walker required much patience on our part. She would have liked to be able to supervise our daily work at the home, so it seemed, and we became increasingly uncertain how long we could work under her domineering authority. The position of juvenile court judge was a joint appointment by the Durham City Council and the county commissioners. The date for the appointment was soon to occur, and we were quite anxious what the outcome would be. She had been the juvenile court judge for many years, and she had announced earlier that she would not seek to be reappointed. But then she had come out and stated that she would seek another term as juvenile court judge. Judge Walker had been a political power in the community, and all indications were that it would be difficult for the politicians to deny her another term in the office. The local media gave the matter considerable attention, and there was considerable speculation who might be appointed to the position if Judge Walker was not chosen for another term. Somehow in the media stirrings over the forthcoming meeting of the city/county officials to decide the matter, my name was one that was mentioned as a possible contender for the job. I never did find out where the news media acquired this information, for I had never expressed any interest in the position. With my name on the possible list of those being considered, I knew if Judge Walker was reappointed, that it would most likely be impossible to work under her for I would be viewed as a political foe of hers! Of course, we were doubtful, anyway, if we could have the patience and fortitude to continue much longer, enduring her authoritarian ways.

The day arrived for the city/county boards to meet, and after some suspenseful moments, the media announced that a local young lawyer had been appointed to the position. Were we ever relieved! I don't know what we would have done if we had resigned our positions at the youth home, in the event she had been reappointed, but we knew it would be most unlikely that we would continue. Later, we were told by Mr. Brame, the chairman of the county commissioners, who had also befriended us and sort of paternalistically adopted us, that the struggle to keep Judge Walker from being reappointed, was the most intense political battle he had experienced in his political career. But thank goodness, the days looked much brighter ahead, for now, the "bread and butter" for seeing us through our Duke days seemed rather well assured! (We must admit, too, that even though the job was confining, we rather liked it. The budget did have allowances in it for us to hire "relief help" from time to time so that we could have time to spend as we chose and be free, momentarily, from Youth Home responsibilities).

Numerous antidotes could be related and mentioned during these days at the Home. We were not especially bothered by children running away, but it did happen from time to time. On one occasion, two of the younger boys ran out of the Home, and Barbara went after them and caught them hiding in an outside, indented corner of the building. She marched them back in the building like a stern school mom! On another occasion, a small boy ran out of the building and took off like a young antelope across the large, open field behind us. I took after him and finally caught him. I was so out of breath that I thought I was going to have a heart attack! The police one night brought in a slightly inebriated adolescent girl. As was our practice, I sent her back with Barbara to the section where she would be assigned a room, but first, she was to take a shower, which we nearly always did as a preventive measure to avoid having head or /body lice invading the Home. While Barbara was looking after her, I completed the entry forms with the police and then went back to see if Barbara had been able to settle her down in her room. Instead, I found that the girl practically had Barbara down in the shower room! The two of us finally were able to get the girl showered and settled for the night!

Some of the children were more lovable than others. We had a young mulatto boy for a week or more, and he was placed in a foster home. We were out playing with the children on the grounds beyond the fenced in part of the yard, and I heard a rustling in the bushes at the edge of the area, and I looked over only to see little George who had been released only that morning. He had run back to the Youth Home hoping, I guess, that he could stay with us. On another day, two of the boys, brothers, who had been in the Home some time before and who had been sent to a state juvenile detention facility, stopped by unexpectedly to see us. We found out that they had come back to Durham to attend the funeral of their mother. We invited them to stay and eat supper with us and tried in a quiet manner to provide some comfort for them. We were humbled to have the trust placed in us that these brothers apparently did.

Periodically, the Grand Jury members came by to inspect the Home as they were required by law to do with penal facilities. Frequently, I was away from the Home when this occurred, and Barbara had to meet with them and show them around by herself. We both suspected that some of the members had some misgivings about two young "Yankees" being in charge of the Home, but nothing was ever said overtly to indicate this. Barbara always handled these inspections with friendly and professional ability. She was much more skilled at doing this, I believe, than I was!

Not long after a new juvenile court judge was appointed, we had purchased a dog for us and the Home. We had looked at these cocker spaniel pups earlier, but thought they were asking more than we could afford. Later, we found out that the owners had come down in the price, and I went to look at them. There were two left from the litter—a blonde one and a rust—colored one. I couldn't decide which one to take, so I received permission to take them both back to the Youth Home and let Barbara and Alice help me make the decision. The blonde one was very active and inquisitive while the rust-colored one was shy and retiring.

If Alice had had her way, we would have taken both of them, but we were not ready to take on the responsibilities for raising two pups. We finally decided on the shy rust-colored pup, and it was not long after I had taken its sibling back to the owners, that he became lively and proved to be quite inquisitive and active. Rusty, naturally, we named him, lived to be seventeen years old and became an integral part of our family.

Usually, I ran errands to town and often stopped by the county manager's office to go over bills and other Youth Home business. Occasionally, Barbara would run some of these errands, and the first time she stopped in at some of the county offices, people said, "You're Mr. Francisco's wife? My, you look young enough to be his daughter!" This happened several times in the first ten to fifteen years of our marriage, and I was never sure just how I wanted to take these remarks. Were they compliments or something else?

We rather frequently entertained friends and some of the faculty at the Home. I kept special account of these occasions and paid for the extra food expenses out of my own pocket and made sure that they were not billed against the Home's budget. One time, we had a distinguished professor as our evening meal guest. He stood behind Barbara's chair at the dining table, and it took a minute or two before we realized he was waiting to seat Barbara. We were not exactly accustomed to some of the eastern/southern folkways! Another time, we invited one of my sociology professors and his family to an evening picnic. We had a comfortable picnic place to the north of the building and enjoyed picnics there. Barbara had made a poppy seed cake; the problem was that it was the time of the year when millions of small tobacco bugs filled the air from the tobacco warehouses across the street. One could not tell if one were eating poppy seeds or tobacco bugs!!

We had been at the Home only a few weeks when we received a phone call from one of the professor's homes that a couple from Drake were at his place, and they wanted to come over and see us. So, on a cold, misty late summer evening, there was a knock at the door, and there stood Bonnie and Lew McNurlen! We both loved to tell this story. We both vaguely knew of each other at Drake, but when we met at the Youth Home door that evening, neither of us were who we thought we were going to be. Neither of us was particularly and favorably impressed with whom we thought we were going to be seeing, and it was a relief to find out we were not these people! That was the beginning of a rich and enduring friendship. The emerging friendship withstood an early test when we went on a picnic to Guilford Courthouse Battlefield Park, and Lew proceeded to analyze the cake that Barbara had made and tell what all was wrong with it!!

The comprehensive departmental examinations I took over a period of several weeks during the summer of 1951 These exams were probably the most important "hurdle" toward meeting the Ph.D. requirements. For Dr. Jensen's part of these exams, I worked all day and part of the next day writing the exam. He permitted me to go to my library carrel and use my portable typewriter for writing the exam, otherwise I might still be writing this exam!! We had to postpone a day of our planned trip to Kitty Hawk over on the Atlantic coast on account of my taking a day longer in writing the exam. We did enjoy the overnight trip to Kitty Hawk for I had the comprehensive exams behind me, and I felt a freedom that I had seldom experienced.

With the main barrier to the doctorate degree behind me, this also changed some other patterns of our living. The way was now open to allow us to start a family, and it was only a matter of a few weeks until we were pregnant. (Yes, I stated "we" for a number of books in the marriage and family area of studies recommended the plural form since meaningful pregnancy does involve both parents!) Several of the other graduate couples in our department talked openly about their becoming pregnant, but we were closed—mouthed about the matter until our pregnancy could no longer be ignored. We had fun in surprising our colleagues.

A new chapter was opening up in our lives, and while excited about this change in the making in our family, we actually took the pregnancy more or less matter-of-fact. Barbara had good medical care at the Duke Hospital, and we gave little thought to the possible complications that a pregnancy could entail. While we thought of ourselves as rather mature individuals, in many ways, I guess we were rather juvenile in realizing the full implications of a pregnancy. Besides, I was quite busy the last full year at Duke and at the Youth Home, for I had received permission from the juvenile court judge to teach three days a week at Wake Forest College. This was about a forty-five minute drive east of Durham. I did hate to leave Barbara at the Youth Home while I did this teaching, but Alice was there with her most of the time I was gone. This made it necessary for Barbara to assume more responsibilities at the Home, so we were both preoccupied with our work. The months passed rapidly . . .

Moving On

*I*t was Father's Day, June 15th, 1952, and I was about to receive
the best Father's Day gift ever. Early that morning, Barbara's
water had broken. As we walked out to get in our car to drive Barbara
to the Duke Hospital, she remarked, "This being a nurse doesn't help at
all!" When we had phoned Bonnie and Lew, who were our stand-by
relief help at that time, without any other remarks, Bonnie replied to the
phone call, "We'll be there!" And they soon arrived to be at the Home
to stay with the one youth who was in detention that morning.

Barbara was only in labor a few hours, and the baby was born—a
boy. Duke Hospital was among the first hospitals to have rooming in
whereby after delivery the newborn baby was moved in the mother's
hospital room where the mother could be with the baby at all times.
Barbara was not yet back from the delivery room, and I had stepped
out of the room for a few minutes; back in her hospital room, I was there
a couple of minutes when I became aware that there was another
being in the room. I looked over toward the baby basket and realized
it was occupied! There lay baby Lee Barton. I went over and looked at
my newborn son, and I had a feeling that defied description. What a
moment! After looking at the new life before me for a while and since
Barbara was still not back, I walked outside to stroll across a part of the
beautiful Duke campus. It was a picture made June Sunday morning,
and as I walked across the campus, I had many thoughts flood my
mind. Barbara and I were now parents, and what an inspiring realization
this was.

Back in Barbara's room, we both took in our new son. It was thrilling
to have the baby right there with us. We named him Lee Barton. We
wanted a short first name that would be difficult to abbreviate and
give him a nickname. Since he was born in North Carolina, the name
"Lee" impressed us as a very suitable name. Barton was the first name
of Barton Stone, one of the early leaders in the Christian Church
(Disciples of Christ) which was the common religious background that

both Barbara's and my family and I shared. Barton Stone also was in numerous ways ahead of his time, in that he was an open—minded and progressive religious leader. His background was one that we liked to have associated with our son's name. Later, we found out that my father did not quite get his new grandson's name correct, and when he phoned Barbara's parents, he told them that we had named Lee, Lee Barton Stone Francisco!! What a memorable Father's Day that June in 1952 was!

I needed to get away where I could concentrate on writing my dissertation in order to complete the final requirements for the Ph.D. degree. So we decided to notify Judge Moore, the juvenile court judge, that we would be leaving the youth home positions on December 15th. We hated to leave Durham and our friends there, but we did want to move ahead on finishing the degree requirements and find a teaching position where we could feel we were pursuing our longer term objectives. So we began preparations for moving from Durham. We would move to Decatur, Illinois, and stay with my parents while I worked on and wrote the dissertation. We purchased a second-hand utility trailer to pack most of our belongings in for the move. We had moved to Durham in one car, but we had begun the process of accumulation where we knew our car could not begin to hold all that we were taking back to Illinois with us.

We packed and packed, and the 15th of December arrived and the trailer was full, and the passenger seat was the only room left in the car for Barbara to sit, hold Lee, put her feet in a dishpan, and have our dog, Rusty, hunched down at her feet in the dishpan! This was one of the few times that I ever saw Barbara cry. When she came out to the car and saw how full it was, (she had counted on space in the back seat to lay Lee down on some blankets, but this was now out of the question). The prospects of a 1,200-mile trip under these conditions were somewhat overwhelming, but we started out, driving slowly and carefully. Only later did we learn that a good friend, who was a part owner in the Plymouth-DeSoto dealer in Durham, had hoped and been working on a plan where one of the Michigan trucks that had brought out a load of cars for his garage, would be able to load us on the auto delivery truck and haul us back most of the way to Illinois. We made frequent stops to air ourselves, and although progress in heading west was somewhat slow, we crept along and traveled about 250 miles the first day!

We soon settled in at my parent's home in Decatur. After the holidays, I resumed work on writing the dissertation by setting up a place in the basement where I could organize and write the data I had collected for the project. I recall how difficult it was to concentrate on my work during the visit of my Aunt Oka and her family and Barbara's parents and brother, George, Jr., during the holidays; I was downstairs writing while I could hear the family upstairs laughing and having a good and relaxed time. How I longed to be upstairs with them, but I held to my determination to work on the dissertation.

My dissertation supervisor, Dr. Hornell Hart, required that I brief (a detailed outline) each chapter that I wrote. Time was running out for the spring deadline for submitting the dissertation if I were to receive the degree in June. I tried to circumvent the briefing of some of the chapters under this pressure, and when I mailed a couple of chapters to Dr. Hart, he responded by writing that these chapters were not nearly as well written as what I had been sending him. He asked, "did you brief these chapters?" The result, I did not receive the degree until a year later than I had hoped to achieve this goal!

When I wanted to take a "break" from the dissertation work, Barbara and I enjoyed walking over to a near by park with our growing young son and carefully pushing him in the swings and other playground equipment. We also went on frequent picnics with my parents to some of Decatur's fine parks. I am sure our living with my parents those late winter and spring months was some imposition on my parents, but they never complained. Barbara did some part—time work at the Decatur-Macon County Hospital, and I did some supply work at churches in the vicinity of Decatur. This brought in some needed cash for us. I don't know if we had arrangements with my parents to help pay grocery bills, but I hope we did have some understanding on how we could help share these expenses. Although Barbara and my father occasionally had some words over how we should be taking care of Lee, the families for the most part had good rapport and a minimum of friction.

In the spring, I looked in to several teaching positions at colleges in West Virginia, Georgia, South Carolina, and Michigan. Positions were offered to me in all these schools (apparently, there was a shortage of sociology professors), but I was in no hurry to accept the offers that were made. Finally in the late spring, I accepted the offer at Albion College, Albion, Michigan. I thought Albion was the college with the most assets to offer. Among the positions I declined was an offer from Paine College in Augusta, Georgia. There, I would not only have been teaching sociology, but I would have also been in charge of a college sponsored social settlement house. I have often wondered what kind of an opportunity this would have been for a somewhat unique experience. Barbara and Lee accompanied me on visits to these campuses, and my parents went with us to Georgia and South Carolina. We combined business and pleasure on these trips.

That summer before moving to Albion, we all took a short vacation and rented a lake cottage on Intermediate Lake near Petoskey, Michigan. Toddler Lee enjoyed splashing around in the shallow water at the edge of the lake. It was an enjoyable several days the family experienced there.

Rental properties in Albion were in short supply, and we ended up renting the upstairs apartment of a house owned by a young couple about our age. They had children, and their boy was about the age of Lee. The apartment was only a couple of blocks from the Albion campus. We looked forward to moving in to this apartment and beginning my teaching career at Albion College.

PART III

"Prof" and Family Life

Families of college professors might be a subculture of their own

Early Teaching and
Home Environments

here were six of us who were new faculty members at Albion in the fall of 1953, and we became good friends of the Branches, Stowells, Cooks, and Hamptons. Later in the year, we went over to the neighboring town of Marshall to eat at the famous Schuler's Restaurant. We were celebrating our completion or near completion of our doctorate degrees. The fellowship was rich and uplifting. We fellows also played golf on a number of occasions, and the camaraderie was great. Bonds of friendship were forming here, some, such as with the Branches, would last the rest of our lives.

As for the teaching, I was young and innocent and did not realize what a heavy load of teaching I was having placed upon me. I was assigned fifteen hours of classroom teaching (twelve hours was common in colleges like Albion), a senior seminar, and supervision of an honors paper. Besides these teaching responsibilities, I was completing the writing of my dissertation. As I look back on those years of teaching, I don't know how I managed all of this. Saturday morning classes were part of the regular schedule, so I had only one and one half day a week free from teaching. In spite of this work, Barbara, Lee, Rusty, and I managed to pack a picnic lunch and go to one of the beautiful roadside parks for an evening picnic on a number of occasions. These picnics were cherished moments.

In the spring, I had managed to complete writing my dissertation. A date was set for me to defend the dissertation before the Duke committee selected to question me about the writing. Barbara, Lee, and I drove out for this final exam. We stayed with our good friends, the Fuquays, the couple of nights we were in Durham. I drove over to the university quite tense and anxious about this oral examination. There were five faculty members on the committee—four from the Sociology Department and one from the Divinity School, Dr. Waldo Beach, who taught Christian Ethics,—my minor field of concentration. One of the first questions asked was by Dr. Hart who asked me the difference between a thesis and a dissertation. I had expected no such question, and I rather stumbled giving my answer. I thought to myself, what kind of questions may be forthcoming that have nothing to do with the subject matter of my dissertation. However, this did not occur, and the ensuing questions were directed toward the content of the dissertation. There was good rapport among the faculty members, and this mood soon spread to me. The examination was passed, and finally the elusive Ph.D. was earned. The next day, I was up in the hall among the offices of sociology faculty, talking with graduate students who were still working on their degrees when Dr. Jensen passed us, paused, and turned around, and remarked "Oh, there is that new Ph.D. My advice to all new Ph.D.'s is to go stick your head in a rain barrel and yell 'doctor' three times and then forget it!" Good advice! His remarks brought me back down to earth!!

The trip back to Albion found me experiencing a kind of freedom such as I had never felt before. It was such a relief to be free of worries and preoccupation about achieving the Ph.D. It was so good to have Barbara and Lee accompanying me, and the bonds of family were never stronger. Barbara had consistently been supportive of my pursuits in graduate work at Duke, and her companionship and understanding were a major factor in seeing the completion of this goal which had been omnipresent throughout our early marriage! She almost earned the degree as much as I did! We practically floated back to Albion!

When we needed a babysitter, we often asked one of my students to come in and stay with Lee. We were near the dormitories, and it was very convenient to call on some of these students. However, on one occasion, we forgot to make arrangements for someone to come in and stay with Lee when we had made plans to drive to Ann Arbor to hear a prominent Methodist bishop speak. It was too late to make babysitting arrangements, so we decided to take Lee with us, who then was past two years old. The bishop was speaking in one of the large, cathedral-like churches in Ann Arbor, and we were seated about halfway down in the sanctuary. We had good friends in Tennessee who raised goats, and we had recently stopped to see them on one of our trips between North Carolina and Michigan, and their goats had made quite an impression on Lee. We had just received word that they would be coming to visit us in Albion. Well, in the middle of the bishop's address, without any warning, Lee yells out, "Tell them to bring the goats!" His voice carried for some distance, and much of the crowded church heard him. I tried to act like I was unattached to the child. We experienced both embarrassment and amusement by the incident. Thereafter, we made sure we had babysitters lined up to stay with the children when we were going out for the evening!

Albion was a somewhat prestigious school, and a number of the faculty had inflated views of themselves and the environment in which they were teaching. This bothered me some, but yet we were content with being there, and we did enjoy the fellowship we experienced with other faculty people. We rather frequently would get together in the evening for varied social activities, and we enjoyed being with these new friends. In the spring of 1955, I was contacted about an opening in sociology at Millikin University in Decatur, Illinois, and after inquiring more into the position, I was offered the job there. This created a difficult dilemma for us. The opportunity to be back in the same city where my parents lived and also back in what you might call my home country (Decatur was only about thirty miles from where I was born) and where my paternal grandmother still lived, was an attraction. Yet Albion was a more bona fide liberal arts college with a much stronger financial base than Millikin. I had considerable difficulty in reaching a decision whether or not to accept the job at Millikin, and I struggled with indecision for several weeks. Barbara did not seem to have any strong preferences concerning staying on at Albion or moving to Decatur and left the decision for me to make. Finally, I said one day, I am going down to the mailbox and send a letter of acceptance to the Millikin offer before I change my mind! And so I did!

We hated to leave our friends at Albion. The Springers, who owned the house in which we rented their upstairs apartment, were among those we were going to miss. Our families were quite compatible, and our children enjoyed playing together. We had had a chance several months earlier to rent a much more attractive apartment and were making plans to move there but then decided we did not want to leave the Springers and canceled plans to move to the more attractive apartment. We had moved our possessions to Albion in the trailer we had moved from North Carolina to Decatur, but a moving van was required to move our belongings to Decatur.

On an earlier trip to Decatur that spring, we had more or less decided to purchase a bungalow—type home with a large yard. But before any final plans were made to purchase this house, my parents had come across a home which they and a good church friend thought was much more suitable for a professor and his family, and they had purchased it for us. We would pay them a nominal amount of rent for the place. This house was an older home, but the interior of it was very comfortable and contained numerous amenities. But it was located on a very small lot and a busy street. We tried not to show our disappointment with their generous purchase for us, but we much preferred the house and location of the house we had planned on buying earlier that spring. I fear our lack of enthusiasm with the place they had purchased was not too well concealed.

The folks wanted to carry out some remodeling in the house, and they had a good friend who was a contractor who remodeled and modernized the kitchen. We also steamed and scraped off the wall paper in the living room (which was quite a job) and made some other improvements in the dwelling. If there had just been a larger yard and we had been located on a less busy street, we would have been much more positive about the place. While all this redecorating was occurring, we stayed with my parents and stored most of our furniture in their double garage.

The stage was now set to begin my teaching at Millikin. I tended to take this new assignment with a more matter-of-fact attitude. I was not nearly as excited about the opening of the school year as I had been at Albion, but the less dramatic beginning, such as no formal convocation as there had been at Albion, was more to my liking. In fact, I had a feeling that I was going to enjoy being on the faculty and that the pressures of being a part of a faculty who had a quite high esteem of themselves, as had been the case at Albion, was going to be a welcome relief!

Newcomers in the Family

*T*hat summer, we spent almost a month in South Miami, Florida, in the new home of my parents' friends who liked to have good friends staying in their home while they were back in Burlington, Iowa, running their beauty academy. We all enjoyed this opportunity to become acquainted with South Florida. Lee absorbed all of this new, different environment in full stride. Lee, my father, and I several times fished in bays of the ocean whenever we could. The weeks there were a wholesome vacation for all the family.

We settled readily in to our new home in Decatur. We fenced in the backyard so Lee could play there with little supervision on our part. The yard was large enough to hold a play yard set, which he enjoyed. School started with ease, and although I still had a rather heavy teaching load, it was not as demanding as my classes had been at Albion. Arrangements had been made with the Methodist superintendent in Decatur, who was a friend of my father, to pastor a small Methodist church in an industrial part of Decatur. We soon learned to love these church people; and John and Wilma Snyder, active members in the church, became lifelong friends.

Dean Miller at Millikin was supportive of the courses I wanted to establish at the school since I was the first full—time sociologist they had had. He advised me to bring before the main academic committee of the faculty the full plans I had for sociology, for he thought the faculty would be more receptive of placing before them the complete curricula I was proposing rather than attempt to have it passed piecemeal. With little difficulty, the committee approved the report I made for the sociology courses. With few exceptions, this was the beginning of creative and congenial rapport I experienced with the faculty.

We came back from Florida with a new one on the way. Barbara was pregnant! We looked forward to an addition to our family. The baby was due toward the end of March. We were so preoccupied with becoming adjusted to living in Decatur and the teaching at the university, that the months passed quickly. However, Becky did not want to wait the full term, and she put in almost a month earlier appearance. On February 29th we commented that we did not believe we were going to have a leap year baby, and as it turned out, she only missed being one by about four hours! The baby was fine, and the delivery was normal. Barbara was only in labor a few hours. My parents looked after Lee while I was at the hospital with Barbara for the delivery. I recall that it was a mild day that seemed more like a spring day than a late winter day. As I looked out the hospital window later in the morning, children were playing nearby without wearing jackets or coats.

We had been preparing Lee for having a new brother or sister, so he was ready for the newcomer when we brought Becky home. I had purchased some new toys for him to receive when we arrived with the new baby, and the transition for him in having a new baby sister went quite smoothly. Barbara and I had been raised as only children, and we definitely wished to have more than one child. We were happy to have our family expanding. It was a great fulfilling feeling for all of us!

Lee started to kindergarten in the late summer of 1957. He walked straight down our street about four blocks to the school he would be attending. I repressed my emotions when I first saw him walk to school, for I knew our ties would never be the same as they had been before he started to school. There would now be other influences entering in to his life. He had a rather strict teacher, and one day, something was said about Barbara having eyes in the back of her head when she would catch him misbehaving. Lee half-believed his mother about her having eyes in the back of her head, but he spoke up and said "Mrs. Hood (his teacher) sure doesn't have eyes in the back of her head!" We don't know what kind of mischief he had been up to that she didn't see!

We enjoyed being close to Findlay where we could easily drive down and see my grandmother. She took great interest in our children, and we were glad that they could have some time with their great—grandmother.

We liked to entertain students in our home. Some Chinese students came in on one occasion and prepared some of their favorite Chinese dishes for our evening meal. We also had faculty in from time to time. The house had an impressive fireplace at one end of the living room, which we seldom used. But on this cool fall evening, we started a fire in it shortly before our faculty guests arrived. The fireplace smoked so intensely that we could soon scarcely see to get around in the downstairs. Hastily, we opened the windows and tried to wave the smoke outside. The smell of smoke was still quite strong yet when our guests arrived! Good fellowship, however, was not sacrificed by this incident that evening. Use of the fireplace after that was postponed until it had had a good cleaning.

I taught summer school the first two summers that I was at Millikin. We were thinking about trying to purchase lake property somewhere in northern Wisconsin or Minnesota, and we needed the extra money that summer school would provide to make this dream a possibility. I didn't mind the extra teaching for I found that something about summer school classes proceeded at a more relaxed pace for teachers and students. In 1956, my parents accompanied us to a two—week vacation into northern Minnesota. The cabin we rented was rather small for four adults and two children, but we found the two weeks a very pleasant time to spend together. Little Becky, who was only six months old, slept in her baby buggy in a crowded hallway between the two bedrooms in the cabin. She seldom fussed, and we could not have asked for a more adjusting baby than she was under somewhat less—than—ideal conditions. Lee tagged his grandfather just about every place he could. Dad enjoyed this tagging, except when it disturbed his fishing. Barbara and I spent much of the time, however, looking around at lake properties—both developed (with cabins on the property) and undeveloped (no cabins on the lakeshore). My father was not too happy with me being gone much of the time looking at properties and missing opportunities to fish with him.

In our covering much of the countryside, looking at lake lots and cabins for sale, we drove down a new country road to us and came across a beautiful crystal blue lake. It seemed especially sparkling and striking, and we stopped and asked a lady working out in her yard near this lake if she knew of any lake property for sale in the area, but she was unaware of any in the vicinity that was for sale. Later, we received information from a realtor in Pequot Lakes about a couple of lots for sale on a lake called Ponto Lake. The following Sunday, our last day of vacationing for the summer in Minnesota, we attempted to find these lots but were unable to find a road that led back to these properties. We stopped at a house on the highway in the vicinity to ask for assistance in how to drive back to these lots. After the man gave us directions for getting back to see these lots, as I often did, I asked if he knew of any other lake property for sale in the area, and he replied that he might sell us some of his lakefront property. We could see no lake from his home and wondered where his lake property was. He said he would take us back to see what he might sell us, so we followed him about one-half mile back behind his house to his lakefront property. It was undeveloped property, and most of it was grown up with brush. However, I was impressed with the potential of his property, and when he told us what he would sell us five hundred feet of the lakeshore for, I knew I was definitely interested in the property.

The next morning, as we were headed back to Des Moines, we stopped by and told this man, whose name was Mr. Oliver, that we would buy the property. I wrote him out a check, and we sealed the transaction with a handshake. We had purchased lake property! What we didn't know then, was that this lake property was on the same beautiful lake we had come upon a few days earlier and thought was such a spectacular and exceptionally attractive body of water. We headed on down to Des Moines where we planned to visit with Barbara's parents and brother before driving on to Decatur. I worried some on the drive down to Des Moines, wondering what we had done. Here we had paid for lake property way up in Minnesota, and now we had no money to make a down payment for any property we might want to purchase wherever I might be teaching in the future. That was the only time I really ever worried about buying this lake property. As it turned out, this was probably, next to deciding to marry Barbara, the wisest decision that I had ever made!

We squeezed in a quick trip to see Bonnie and Lew McNurlen in Durham before school started at Millikin. While in Durham, I expressed interest in buying a station wagon soon which would be of great help as we built a cabin on the lake property, and before I knew it, Lew had me down at the Ford dealer in the midst of buying a new Ford wagon. Lew's unusual abilities to pull off unusual business deals, got the car salesman to come down to a price which I could scarcely refuse. So we left Durham, driving back home in a new Ford station wagon. Now we had lake property and a station wagon to facilitate building a cabin, but no money left to actually start building next spring. Barbara was consulted in all these transactions, and as she usually did, she agreed to what I was doing. Actually, she was about as excited about what we were doing as I was!

That school year, I must confess, I did much daydreaming about getting started in the spring with building a cabin on the lakeshore of this Minnesota lake. Sometimes my dreams turned a little grandiose, and I imagined building an elaborate summer cottage. Daydreams or not, it was exciting to think about the lake project after school was out in the coming spring. We only spent a couple of weeks then the next summer at the lake where I did some clearing of brush with a powered brush cutter that I borrowed from Mr. Oliver. We did no actual building but did proceed to line up arrangements for construction of the cabin.

The next school year, our attention was distracted from the cabin building to preparing for a further expansion of our family. Barbara was pregnant, and we were expecting a new baby some time in late February or March. That year I was filling the pulpit at a neighboring village, and as the time of the new one's arrival approached, we worked out some signals in case the baby was coming during the church services, whereby I would know to cut the service short and hasten home or to the hospital. Thankfully, we did not have to put into operation these signals or plans! Susan Lois arrived on March 5th. The other children had been earlier than the expected date, and we assumed that Susan would also arrive earlier. But she took her time in coming, and we waited out a few anxious days for her birth. The day she was born, unlike the time when Lee and Becky put in their appearance, we took our time getting to the hospital. In the late morning, we were rather sure that the birth was imminent, but we did not arrive at the hospital until mid or late afternoon. I guess by now we were beginning to feel like veterans in having babies. While Barbara was in labor, her obstetrician and I watched a Disney film in the obstetrics waiting room. He would go back to the delivery room to check on Barbara and then come back to continue watching the Disney production. This was before the days when fathers were allowed to come in to the delivery room and observe the actual birth.

Lee had prepared Becky for the coming home of the newcomer by telling her that they would receive presents when we brought the baby home from the hospital. Fortunately, we had prepared for this and had presents on hand for them. Now our family numbered five, and we were thankful to have three healthy children. Actually, we had given little thought to the babies being anything else than healthy, and I fear we would have been poorly prepared if one of them had possessed some abnormalities.

That fall, I was to officiate at the wedding of my student assistant in Danville, Illinois. We left Lee and Becky with my parents. I can still see toddler Becky going up the steps of my parents' home in an unquestioned manner of trust as we left them with my folks. At the wedding rehearsal dinner, baby Susan was fussy, and I recall carrying her in my arms and taking her outside to soothe and quiet her crying. I felt perfectly at home in doing this, and it felt exhilarating to be holding my baby daughter in my arms. Ah, being a father was rewarding beyond words, and Barbara felt the same way about being a mother. Newcomers were entering our family, and we both were grateful for the untold opportunities that lay ahead for us as parents and a family!

Discouragement and Promise

*P*ressure was being placed upon me by the director of the summer school program at Millikin to teach during the summer school sessions. This disturbed me for I did not wish to continue summer school teaching now that we had purchased lake property with the previous two summers of teaching; I wanted to work on developing our lake property and enjoy our summers at the lake in Minnesota. Furthermore, while I liked being at Millikin, I felt that I was in a dead—end situation there with few prospects of any kind of advancement. So when a phone call came from Dean Leffler at Albion about returning to Albion, it was tempting. The salary he offered me was not enough more than I was earning at Millikin to increase my interest in returning to Albion, but Albion had a good pension plan which Millikin did not have at that time. However, I turned down the offer to return to Albion.

A few days later, Dean Leffler phoned back, and while he said they could not pay moving expenses, he could make a somewhat better salary offer. I accepted. This turned out to be a mistake. But I did not know this at that time.

My parents were quite disappointed to know that we would be leaving Decatur. In fact, we were told later that Dad canceled some plans for improvement (especially for the children) that he was going to make. But we were ready for a change, and Albion seemed to present the opportunity for challenges that I did not see occurring at Millikin.

So back to Albion we moved in the late summer of 1959. It almost felt like we were burning up the road between the two communities with moving vans! Rental housing was still in short supply in Albion, and we had ended up renting a house that looked quite run—down on the outside but was quite livable on the inside. The owner was a rather eccentric lady who lived across the highway from the house we were renting. Also another attraction to renting this house was that it was only two blocks from the Albion campus. We stayed the first couple of nights with the Swans, my colleague in sociology who was now department chairman. As soon as some interior painting was done inside the house by a relative of the landlady and as soon as the moving van arrived with our furniture, we moved into the house. It was roomy, and with Barbara's charming talents, it was made quite comfortable. The stage was set for a second round of teaching and living in Albion.

We soon found out that we had changed, and our friends at Albion had changed in the intervening years we had been at Millikin. One could say that we had become more cosmopolitan in our perspectives while they still were somewhat circumscribed by a private, somewhat in-grown prestigious college. They seemed even more firmly influenced by this environment than they had been before. We enjoyed having fellowship with them, but there was not the rapport with them that there had been. Also the teaching schedule remained heavy and stressful. One new factor developed that countered much of this feeling on our part. We became active in a newly formed Quaker group that met on Sundays at the Jackson YWCA. We had never actually worshipped with a Quaker group before, and we found their silent worship quite meaningful. One Sunday, we were invited to have dinner in one of the Quaker family homes who had also invited some visiting guests from the Ann Arbor Quaker Meeting. One of these guests was a professor at the University of Michigan, and I asked him what subject he taught at the university. Later, to my great embarrassment, I found that he was an internationally renowned economist. From then on, I attempted to avoid such blunders!

Albion drew students from wealthy Detroit suburbs and North Shore palatial homes from the Chicago area. One student who enrolled in some of my classes was from one of these wealthy families, and he was about the most class-conscious individual I had ever known. He did seem to be at ease in my company, and one day, he asked me if I lived in this run-down appearing house down the street, and when I replied "yes," he said, "I was afraid you did!"

Barbara, though, loved living in this "run-down appearing" house. While, as previously mentioned, the interior was very livable, it was old, such that she did not have to worry about our children damaging the place. There were a number of small children in the neighborhood, and our place was often the gathering place for the children to come and play with our children. Sometimes there would be six or eight small children in our yard or inside in a large room that we used as a play room. Barbara loved to have these children at our place and direct their play and frequently have refreshments for them.

The second year there, Albion's president had retired, and a new president came to fill the vacant position. Dr. Swan and his wife invited the new president and his wife for dinner and asked us on short notice to come too. We had already made plans to be with our friends for a social gathering, and we declined the invitation. This did not go over well with the Swans and was one incident of several that indicated growing estrangement with the Swans. Just before the adjournment of an evening faculty meeting, Swan came to me and said he would like to see me in our office after the meeting. I met him in the office we shared, and he said Albion was not big enough for both of us, and that since I was the younger man, that I should prepare to leave Albion. In some ways, this announcement surprised me, and in other ways, I was not surprised. I did not argue with him or further discuss the matter. In fact, this was the last conversation I had with Swan, and we never spoke to one another again. Of course, I did not feel comfortable with this kind of behavior with an individual whom I once had considered a good friend, but I fear at that time I was not a big enough character to attempt to achieve some kind of reconciliation. Soon afterward the new president of the college called me in and in a matter-of-fact way said he understood that Swan wanted me to leave, and he said my employment would be terminated at Albion by the end of the following year. Again, I did not discuss the matter with the president, but accepted his authority without question. I was rather fed up with Albion, and the sooner I could find other employment, the better. I also knew that Swan had his eye on the vacant position of the dean of the college, and he had been "buttering up" the new president, hoping he would be appointed to this position.

Of course, I was upset some by this happening, but at the same time, it decided for me to leave Albion as soon as I found a desirable teaching position. Barbara, being the "trooper" that she was, steadily stood by me during this crisis. Her companionship and understanding certainly eased the stress of those moments. Also, I had several teaching opportunities in the making, and I was not too worried but what I would find new employment without too much trouble. While I had the margin of another year of staying at Albion if I chose to do so, I had no intention of remaining there any longer than I had to do so! In retrospect, the whole incident was a good learning experience for us, for our lives previously had rolled along smoothly—probably too smoothly—, and now our peace and quiet had really been disturbed.

Among the schools where there was a good possibility of being offered a position was a state school in Oklahoma. The president of this university phoned me at least twice and attempted to interest me in coming there. I was interested, but we were not too enthusiastic about moving to Oklahoma. I was much more interested in a position at Lycoming College in Pennsylvania. Actually, I had been offered a position there two years earlier when I accepted the offer to come back to Albion. We had not visited the Lycoming campus before, and they asked me to come out for interviews. Through a good faculty friend at Millikin who had friends in the Methodist education headquarters in Nashville, I had found out that Lycoming was considered by Methodist educators as one of their most promising colleges.

That spring, before the encounter with Swan, I had been working on a project that I felt had promise. I was drafting a plan whereby the college where I might be teaching would sponsor a series of informal meetings centered around in-depth considerations of what was involved in democratic living. This would include not only political pursuits and programs, but democratic living throughout the range of individual and community living. We would invite to the campus individuals of note to come for several days where we would sit around a conference table and have faculty and students introduce topics related to democratic living and discuss among us, under the direction of me, the presenting faculty member, and/or groups of students the subject matter that had been introduced. I and others who knew about the project were enthusiastic about its potential.

We drove out to visit the Lycoming campus. My parents accompanied us, and we made the trip out there and back a pleasant one. I recall little Becky frequently asking us, "Are you happy?" Also, in one of the restaurants on this trip, Lee was acting up, and Becky leaned over and said to her brother, "Daddy says, no, no!": It was a rather fun trip, and visiting some of Pennsylvania was a new experience for us. We liked the people we met at the college, and the feeling seemed to be mutual. The college officials liked the project on democratic living on which I was working on and said they thought it could be just the kind of program the college could support. We were again offered the position in sociology there, and I accepted the offer. So in the late forthcoming summer, we would be moving to Pennsylvania—a new environment for us.

Living a Full Life

*I*n the summer of 1961, we made a trip to Williamsport to search for a place to live. We ended up renting a large two-story brick house that had been the home of a prominent family. Actually, the house had a partly finished third floor with steps that led up to a look-out type roof platform. Later, I found out that Lee made a dash to get up there to the look-out and explore the set up. From there, one could see much of the surrounding area of Williamsport. I guess Lee anticipated that his father would declare this place off-limits, and he wanted to get up there before this regulation was made! He was correct in knowing that I would put it into effect. The slate roof was steep and angled off in different directions, and there was only a small guard rail around the look-out. It would be rather dangerous to be up there, but Lee was determined to look over the situation before the children were forbidden to be up there. So far as I know, no other family member ever made it up there during the seven years we lived in Williamsport. The house did promise to be a very comfortable, roomy place for us, and it was near Lycoming College. We drove back to Albion and began to pack for the moving van to move our possessions to Williamsport. We would not accompany the moving van in the moving process. One of the faculty wives had graciously volunteered to oversee the carrying in to the house of our belongings when the moving van arrived. After the van left Albion, we drove out to the lake property in Minnesota.

Again, our parents joined us at our place, and we enjoyed the fellowship with them. Our dads really found each other's company meaningful and refreshing, and when they were together, we had to keep an eye on them for they would come up with ideas of improvements they would like to make on the cabin or grounds that we might prefer to turn thumbs down on! Joking aside, we all liked this time together, and the lake property was turning out to be a real godsend for the family. We were giving some consideration to having a small cabin moved in for our parents to take turns staying in during the weeks they were at the lake. We thought this would even add more to the pleasures of the place if we could accomplish this. Dad and I especially looked into several possibilities, and toward the end of summer, we ended up buying a cabin across the lake which would be rather ideal for a guest cottage—especially for the parents to fix up to their tastes. We arranged for a building moving business to move the cabin, and our neighbor, Otto Hanes, was willing to supervise the moving in of the dwelling. We would have had to return to Williasmsport before this could be done, so we appreciated the assistance of our neighbor.

I started out the school year at Lycoming by having hernia surgery at the Williamsport Hospital. James Tong, who had been a student at Millikin, came and stayed with the family while I was recuperating from the surgery. I was able to meet my classes at the beginning of the fall semester. The teaching load was more manageable than it had been at Albion and Millikin. We soon fell in love with the country around Williamsport. The city was nestled in the Susquehanna River Valley, and the Allegheny Mountains were all around us. Whenever possible, we took rides up through the mountains and explored new scenes and new drives. Truly, we were in the midst of a beautiful country.

During the summer, my parents told us that my father would be retiring from the First Christian Church in Decatur, and they would like to move to Williamsport to be near us if that was satisfactory with us. Of course, we said it would be fine. I think Barbara had some reservations about this, but she never verbalized them. She no doubt had misgivings about them interfering with our family affairs. But no great problems developed, and we experienced good rapport with them. The minister of the large downtown Methodist church met my father at a ministerial association meeting and soon approached him about being an assistant at the Methodist church. Dad accepted the offer to do this, and this position, mostly calling on the ill and families in the church facing various problems, worked out to the satisfaction of Dr. Ake, the Methodist minister, and Dad. Dr. Ake did not especially care for the pastoral responsibilities of calling on people, and Dad greatly enjoyed this activity. We found my parents an apartment close by, and at the end of the school year, the downstairs of a duplex directly across the street from us opened up, and Dad and Mom rented it. Certainly, they were handy when we needed someone to stay with the children when we were going to be gone. I feared we took their "babysitting" services too much for granted and did not often express to them our appreciation for helping us out.

We entertained in our home several single faculty members, including two single women and one single man faculty. We frequently packed a picnic lunch, and often, the two ladies accompanied us on these picnics. There were several beautiful picnic places where we went. One was up the scenic Lycoming Creek Valley. The fellowship with these people was greatly appreciated.

The project I had been working on back at Albion to establish a center for the study of democratic living progressed promisingly, and by the second year, we held our first session. We invited to the campus a number of individuals who had been recommended by the Lycoming staff and local residents for three to four days of conversation on a variety of subjects related to democratic living. Faculty members that I asked to lead different discussions fully cooperated, and the session was well received by both our guests and faculty. From there on, such sessions were held once or twice each semester. Later, we also invited senior students to come in and lead some of the discussions, and this added much to the program. The project was exciting and full of promise.

For some time, Barbara and I had considered adopting a child. Ever since we had been at the juvenile detention home in Durham and seen children sent to large state youth institutions who we believed need not have been taken to such impersonal environments, we had said that if we ever had the chance, we would like to adopt a child and avoid the child being placed in such institutions. We had looked into such possibilities while in Michigan, and we continued our interest in this matter after we moved to Pennsylvania. But time moved on, and one day, I said to Barbara that I was fearful that this dream was not going to materialize as we were becoming older, and the realities of adopting a child became a more remote possibility. Less than a week after I had said this to Barbara, we received a phone call from the Pennsylvania Children's Aid Society, an adoption agency with whom we had been consulting, that they had a little Indian boy lined up in the Dakotas that we might want to consider taking into our home. An appointment was made to drive down to Philadelphia to the home office of this agency and find out more about this Indian boy. So soon, we took our children and drove to Philadelphia to talk with case workers there about the matter.

We found out that the child was eight—eights Sioux Indian and had been living as a foster child with a Caucasian family out in South Dakota. His biological mother was so limited in resources that she was unable to keep all her children and had had two of them placed in foster homes. The foster mother's health was failing, and although they would have liked to keep the six-year-old Indian boy, her health condition was going to force her to give him up. We were definitely interested in what we were told in Philadelphia, and the agency made arrangements for us to drive on out and meet the boy. Soon after arriving at our lake property in Minnesota, we made plans to drive on to South Dakota and meet the Indian boy. We were all excited about the prospects which were developing.

We left early from our cottage on Ponto Lake to drive out to South Dakota to meet the Indian boy. The social worker there had arranged for us to meet him soon after our arrival. We spent the rest of the afternoon getting acquainted with him. We went to a city park, and Philip, his name, played with our children, and we soon felt a bond forming with him. Philip went back to stay with his foster parents, and we went to a motel for the evening. There was a possible complication that placed some anxious moments for Barbara and me. There was a possibility that Barbara was pregnant. We were looking forward to having a fourth child, but not two more. To our great relief, however, Barbara's period commenced the next day, and we knew she was not pregnant. So we were able to have a more free and open feeling developing toward Philip.

The full day we spent with Philip in South Dakota was an emotionally fulfilling day as we increasingly felt warm ties developing with him. Never will I forget when we crossed a street and he put his small hand in mine in a trusting manner that touched me in a warm and reassuring way that we were doing the right thing. The next morning, we left with Philip to return to our Ponto Lake home. Philip seemed to relate to all of us in a very wholesome manner. We stopped at a town on the way back and purchased a pair of swimming trunks for him, for we knew he would want to wade in the lake and join our children as they splashed around in the water.

When we arrived back at the lake, more of our family members were there than I think there ever was or would be at one time. My parents were there, Barbara's parents and her brother were there, Barbara's cousin and her family of five were there, and as I recall, one of my aunts and her husband were also there. How Philip was able to keep everyone straight is a marvel, but he seemed to do so. It would have seemed that the small child would have been overwhelmed!

By the time we left Ponto at the end of the summer, Philip was well integrated in to the family, and it was a good feeling having him with us as we drove back to Pennsylvania. He had not attended school, and after thinking through the matter, we decided to enroll him in kindergarten even though he could have been placed in the first grade. We did not want him to feel under pressure at school as he became adjusted to his new home and new environment. Barbara and I believed that this was a wise decision.

The more individuals in a group, families included, the more complicated human relationships are supposed to become. Social integrationists have drawn diagrams graphically showing how this happens. Bringing Philip into our family did not especially seem to bring this about in our family. We did observe how Susan, more or less, became his mentor, and what Sue liked, Philip liked; and what she disliked, he followed. This was true with many of his food tastes.

Early on, Becky and Sue became close to one another and became constant playmates as they were growing up. One of them was always, so it seemed, thinking up new ideas of what to do and what to play. At our cabin, as they were a little older, they had numerous hide-outs at the edge of the woods that surrounded our grounds. At home in Williamsport, blanket tents, toys, and other objects representing imaginary dwellings were often scattered all over the large entrance way and the living room. One incident that stands out is how they planned their own Christmas Eve pageant to present to the family. It was quite creative what they had planned and performed.

Even more interesting for Barbara and me to watch was how Lee's pattern of picking on Becky changed as Susan became older. Lee had liked to belittle Becky, calling her stupid, dumb, etc. But for some reason, when the girls were about five and seven, he began to turn his attention to Sue and attempt to make her feel inferior. But Sue was another personality, and she did not accept in the passive manner that

Becky had been doing, when her brother's tormenting turned on her. She could dish it right back to Lee. Lee had found his match in Susan. Since Barbara and I had been raised as only children, we were quite interested in how the siblings treated one another and related to each other. While we were not aware of ever being seriously overwhelmed with raising four children, we did find the experience challenging and consuming. Being a sociologist, I had thought that I would keep extensive notes on their development and interaction patterns, but I soon abandoned this idea for I just wanted to enjoy participating in the raising of a family of four alert, creative, and lovable children!

PART IV

Life on the Changing Stage

If anything is certain, it is change.
Inwardly and outwardly, life changes.

North Country, Here We Come!

*C*hanges in administration officials at Lycoming were affecting the creative and challenging environment in which I had been working. College funds had been cut off for the Center for Study of Democratic Living, and with some assistance from former participants, we raised funds for the last year this project was in operation. Fundraising was not my "cup of tea," and this development was distasteful. Also, the faculty was being divided by the new dean, with about half supporting him in the policies he was wanting to initiate at the college and about half were strongly opposing to his aggressive efforts to prevail with his proposed changes.

During the holidays of 1967-1968, Lee flew with me to Duluth-Superior to be interviewed about a sociology position at the University of Wisconsin-Superior. It was an attractive position, and although I did not accept the offer right then, I told the UWS people I would give the matter serious consideration. After several weeks of thinking about the matter and, after discussing it with Barbara and the family, I phoned and accepted the offer. Soon after my acceptance, I went downtown in Williamsport and purchased a warm winter coat, for we were moving to North Country!!

We really were reluctant to move from Williamsport. We liked very much living there. Our children had friends there, and Lee had his first serious girlfriend, that made it difficult for him to leave. But conditions at the college had become bitter and extremely unpleasant as a place to teach. While I said there is no utopian place to live, there had to be better environments in which to work in than what had developed at the college there.

The strain was such in leaving Williamsport that I felt some interim project that would absorb our attention before the new school year commenced in Superior might be beneficial for all of us. Earlier, we had made inquiries about directing a project for the American Friends Service Committee. After correspondence and interviews with people at AFSC, we were hired to direct one of their work projects in a low—income area of Indianapolis, Indiana. Barbara and I drove down to Pendle Hill, a Quaker conference and retreat center in a suburban community of Philadelphia, for a two—day training session for those who were going to direct various work projects for AFSC. The social and spiritual atmosphere at Pendle Hill made a strong, positive impression on Barbara and me, and I hoped sometime in the future that I might be able to spend a sabbatical in this inspiring place and do some of the writing that I had been wanting to pursue. Unfortunately, this never materialized.

Back home in Williamsport, final preparations were made for moving our belongings to Superior. Lee and I had driven a U-Haul truck, in which we had most of my parents' furniture, out to Superior soon after school was over for the year. While in Superior, we rented an apartment for my parents, and we purchased an older, but comfortable house for us. My parents would supervise the unloading of the moving van at our newly purchased house while we went to Indianapolis. Then they would drive on to Ponto Lake, meet Barbara's folks there, and spend the rest of the summer there.

Lee and I went back to Williamsport on the bus. It was a cold, rainy, dreary day when we departed from Superior, and when the bus went along the waterfront of the bay off Lake Superior, the bay and shoreline seemed to exaggerate the dreariness of the landscape, and I thought about what kind of a place was I bringing my family to live. It certainly did not reveal any of the beauty then that surrounded Williamsport. I had a rather despairing feeling grip my stomach. I felt it would be easy to feel that I had made a mistake to move to Superior. (Thank goodness this feeling was short—lived.)

After the moving van had departed, we pulled out from our home of seven years, and our heartstrings were pulled as various neighbors came out to wave good—bye to us. Except for the problems at the college, it had been a wonderful experience living in this city, nestled in the beautiful Allegheny Mountains, and we were breaking the ties that not only had endeared us to our neighborhood, but also numerous other bonds that had developed with a variety of groups of people that meant much to us. We humans do pay a price for our mobility!

We arrived in Indianapolis in the later afternoon and quickly arranged for sleeping in the house that had been arranged for part of our group to stay in. We had two college assistants to help us in the project. The young lady, Sally, a home economics major, was to be in charge of the food, and the young man was to help supervise the activities with which the students would be involved. Barbara, Philip, and the girls stayed upstairs; and Lee, Dave,—the male student assistant, and I prepared make-shift beds to sleep downstairs. All hours of the night, so it seemed, individuals from Mayer Settlement House— our headquarters for the project—, kept bringing in students who were arriving at various terminals. It was like trying to sleep in Grand Central Station! It was a good introduction to the public living, which would occur for the next seven to eight weeks.

The next day, the project assistants were busy preparing another house, about three blocks away from us, for most of the students to stay there. The students were of high school age, and most of them came from quite prominent families. As I recall, there were nineteen students in the project. Local Quakers and the people at the Mayer Settlement House (about two blocks from the house we were staying in,) were very helpful in seeing that we secured basic items and assisting us in setting up our spartan living arrangements.

Projects had been set up for us to do, such as painting houses, supervising play lot games, community organizing, etc. Some of our group incurred the wrath of a local councilman with their community organizing, and at an open public meeting, some of them displayed their "parliamentary skills" by "walking all over" (so to speak) the councilman with their motions, amendments, etc., at this public meeting. Of course, this did not endear our group any more to the councilman!

As implied, these were exceptionally bright students, who at the high school level, were reading books that I assigned to college seniors. Oh my, I thought, what a challenge it would be to have college classes like this, or would it be more than I would wish to attempt to direct? The students in the evening tended to string out along the sidewalk that led from the house where we were staying and where the meals were served, as they walked down to the Mayer Settlement House. One evening, Barbara and I and a few students were bringing up the rear when some people sitting on their front porch motioned for me to come up that one of the men wanted to speak with me. He wanted to know if I was in charge of this group of young people, and I wondered, "Oh boy, what is he going to say?" But when I responded that I was more or less in charge of the group, he declared, "I just wanted to tell you that they are the finest group of youth that I have ever seen!" Such an unqualified compliment, I had not expected.

Few days passed without some kind of excitement and drama. The weeks passed quickly. At the end of the project, residents in the neighborhood had an appreciation potluck supper for our group at the Mayer Settlement House. These people in this low—income area of Indianapolis seemed really to be grateful for the varied ways in which we related with them. It was a very moving experience.

How our children were affected by being a part of this project, I am not sure. Through the years, Barbara and I received varied responses from them about how the Indianapolis experience had influenced them. Barbara and I, I know, were exhausted at the end of the project for we were involved about eighteen hours a day, or so it seemed, with developments that demanded our attention. The experience made an indelible mark upon us—for the good, I hope. It certainly took our minds off the transition we were making in moving from Williamsport to Superior. We gained even more respect for the American Friends Service Committee and for Quakers, for while they held us to a tight budget, they were quite wonderful and congenial people with whom to work with. It was a relief, though, to drive on out to Ponto Lake and relax there for several days before school began in Superior.

Back in Superior, I found out that I had read the calendar incorrectly, and school started sooner than I had expected. I was phoned from the university by the chairman and told the department was meeting, and he wondered where I was! I hurried and drove over to the university, and it was embarrassing to walk late into my first meeting. Also, I had counted on several more days to complete preparations for my classes before school started, and consequently, I was not well prepared to meet some of my classes. I was not getting off to a good start for the school year. But it was not too long before the teaching pace settled down for me, and responsibilities at the university began to proceed at a more normal and less hectic course. The people with whom I was working with were congenial, and the dean of the university seemed understanding and supportive of my breaking in to a new educational environment.

Although I thought Barbara would like our new home that Lee and I had purchased earlier, I also felt that I was taking a chance without her being there when we selected the house that we chose. Fortunately, she liked it. There was a large kitchen with plenty of cupboards, and this feature naturally appealed to her. The neighbors next to us had voluntarily mowed our yard, which was an indication of the friendly and helpful people among whom we would be living. As it turned out, we would be living in this house for the next twenty-three years—the longest we had ever lived in one place. My parents liked the apartment that we had rented for them, but they indicated that it was a little small for them, and at the end of the school year, they found close by a much larger apartment which they rented and soon moved in to and with which they were more comfortable.

One of the first winters we lived in Superior, we had several blizzards. Our house faced the northeast, and when these blizzards blew in off Lake Superior, our house was really plastered with snow, even though it was shielded by spruce trees on three sides. The snow piled up so deeply that drivers acquired little orange balls to put on the antennas of their cars so that one could be seen as they came to street corners where the snow banks were so high that one could not be seen otherwise, until out in the middle of intersections.

Yes, we really were in North Country. We thought that this must be normal for Superior winters, but we found out that such severe winter storms were really not that common.

The Ordeal of Change

$\mathcal{T}$he fellowship and bonds of love that permeated our family were not unnoticed by Barbara and me. I recall when we would be sitting out in front of our Ponto Lake cottage during the ecumenical services that we held back at our place during the summer months that I would think that this priceless fellowship with Barbara's parents and my parents will begin to come to an end one of these days before long, for our parents were reaching ages where their life expectancies were growing shorter. How fortunate we were, I knew, to have the kind of endearing relationships among all of us that we experienced. Such I feared many families could not assert, that they were able to enjoy. How extremely fortunate we were.

Early in 1973, Bertha, Barbara's stepmother (although none of us ever thought of her as a stepmother, she was so completely integrated into the family), found out she had pancreatic cancer. Within a few short months, she died. The next year, Barbara's father became ill, and by mid-summer, he died. Our revered and valued friend and neighbor (and my mentor teacher at Drake) held both funerals back in Des Moines. Then my father was diagnosed with cancer in late 1976, and although he lived longer than his doctor predicted he would, Dad died in the early winter of 1978. Mother stayed with us until arrangements were made for her to rent an apartment in a retirement complex in Superior. While out at Ponto with us in early 1980, she suffered a series of strokes and died in July of that year. Mother's services were held outside at our place on Ponto Lake. I am thankful that while they were all living, that I more or less imprinted indelible images of them present with us at the Sunday morning ecumenical services and in other settings. Precious memories, indeed!

Lee met Lori in high school and began to date her more seriously. In a couple of years, they were engaged, and plans were made for their wedding in June 1974. Dad helped in the wedding ceremony at Lori's home church in Superior. It seemed, in a rather short time, Lee was heading out on his own, and the family was further shrinking. Becky also was signaling that wedding bells were not far away, and in the summer of 1977, she and John were married, with Dad officiating at their wedding. Adjusting to these changes in our family was not exactly easy. But almost overnight, so it seemed, our children had grown up, and they were beginning the process of charting their own courses. The ordeal of change was well under way in our family!

James, the student from the Far East, now residing in Washington, D.C., and who had become a good friend of the family, indicated he would come see us sometime at our Ponto Lake cottage. In the summer of 1977, he arrived in an old car that had cost him some repairs as he drove out to see us. He was broke when he arrived. It was good to see Jim, and we welcomed him to our summer home. Not long after he arrived, he announced that he would be staying with us for the foreseeable future. We were, in many ways, Jim's American home. This was when my father was ill, and I foresaw a trying year ahead with Dad's illness. So when Jim announced that he would be staying on, I didn't know if I had reserve powers to deal with mounting complexities in our family life. My psychic and spiritual limitations I felt were being tested! I think Barbara felt somewhat the same way, but with all the people that were still around, we did not have a good opportunity to talk with one another very thoroughly about the new development of having Jim in our home for some length of time. But we both decided to make the best of the situation. We proceeded to get him settled in the basement room back home where Lee had been staying before he was married. We found out that Jim had some eccentric characteristics which we were never sure were more related to his different Asian cultural background or were just personal idiosyncrasies. While there were some strains for us in having Jim living with us, for the most part, our relationships with him were wholesome and creatively challenging for us. Barbara, however, bore the brunt of the adjustments that were required, and for the most part, she accepted his presence in a constructive and positive manner. At the end of the school year, Jim announced he was returning to Washington, D.C. We think he was expecting us to coax him into staying longer, but we didn't. Apparently, our failing to attempt to persuade him to stay insulted him, for he quietly left, and we never heard very often from him after his departure. We hated this for we liked Jim, but I fear we did not understand him very well. He was somewhat an enigma to us.

When we went to the Ponto Lake cottage, we always had some of the children or family with us. One week, early in the spring, no one accompanied us to Ponto. I felt that just Barbara and me there without the children would be undesirable, and I was not especially looking forward to this change. But to my pleasant surprise, it was a great week. How enjoyable it was not to have any family interruptions. Of course, it was good to have some of our children with us at Ponto, but we also discovered that being there without any of them was also quite pleasant.

Sue graduated from the University of Minnesota School of Forestry, and early in her forestry career, she worked at various forestry jobs—often Native American forestry reservations. At one of these jobs, she met a young forester from southern Wisconsin, and it soon became evident that they had interests in one another that transcended just being coworkers in their forestry employment. After some time of learning to know one another much better, they planned to marry, and they asked me to perform the wedding down at Craig's home town of Clinton, Wisconsin. So in July of 1982, we drove down to Clinton for the wedding. Lee and Mollee rode down with us. Yes, we now had a granddaughter, in fact, two granddaughters—Nikkee,—Lee and Lori's baby who prevented Lori from attending the wedding. Well, do I recall Mollee wanting to take in fully her aunt Sue's wedding. The wedding was outdoors at Craig's home, and young Mollee parked herself on the front row of the chairs that had been arranged, for she was going to be sure that she missed nothing that would take place in the ceremony. The experience of officiating at the wedding of our youngest daughter was an event that I shall never forget. Further change was occurring in our family, but this was one of those changes welcomed by our family.

In a few short years, so it seemed, major changes had taken place in our family. Our parents had died, our three children had married, Becky and her husband had divorced, we had adopted a fourth child, we had two granddaughters born—soon to be followed with the birth of three more granddaughters, a former student had moved into our home and lived with us for nearly a year, we took in a high school—aged boy whose family had disintegrated (a concerned older student in one of my classes had influenced us to take this boy and have him live with us for several months), I had taken on the responsibilities of being president of the board of directors of a long established mission for treating chemically dependent individuals which lasted for twelve years, etc. Time never dragged for Barbara and me. And now, a new challenge was looming on the horizon. Retirement was just around the corner!

Early Retirement Years

arly in the school year of 1987-1988, I went to the head of our division and let her know that I was planning to retire at the end of the school year. She was not too glad to hear this but did not attempt to change my mind. I requested no big retirement parties or any special publicity about my retirement for I did not care for much fuss being made over me. So at the end of the school year, a small group of faculty friends had dinner with me at a nearby dining facility, and this recognition was really all I wished to have. There was also a coffee and refreshments for me on my office floor near the end of the semester. I did teach a class that summer, one of the few times I had taught in the summer session, in order to have the base for my state pension increased. I rather enjoyed this closing class session, for summer school classes usually seem to be more relaxed than classes are during the regular school year.

Clearing out my office after twenty years of teaching at Superior was a major effort. I knew I had accumulated many items and stored them in my office, but not until we began to pack and sort through all the clutter did I realize how much I had crowded into the finite office space. I could scarcely believe that the office could hold all that it did. Barbara, when she could, assisted me in this activity. I took numerous boxes of books, papers, reports, etc., home and threw away box after box of superfluous items. The hallway outside my door was lined with these boxes of unwanted materials. The janitor, who was a good friend, I am sure sighed several times when he came the next time and saw the line up of boxes in the hallway. Except for one other office in the building, I believe my office had been the prize—winning one for accumulation and clutter!

Earlier I had found out that remodeling our cottage at Ponto and making it into a year—around dwelling would not be as expensive as I had thought it would be. So we began to inquire into various construction firms about engaging in this work. We finally decided upon having a full ground floor excavated and put under the existing structure and making only a few changes in the original dwelling. We were rather sentimental about our cottage of thirty-two years, with all the memories associated with it, and we wished to keep it as much as possible like it was. Besides, we had decided we did not want to tie up a large sum of money from our retirement funds on erecting a new home or including many "frills and fancies" in the remodeling project. We wished to be able to engage in other activities, such as travel, during the retirement years. We planned, though, to have a comfortable, practical, and livable house for our year—around home at Ponto.

Selling our house in Superior turned out to be more difficult than we had planned upon. The house was heated by a coal furnace and stoker, and we thought this might have some appeal for potential buyers. Since we had recently experienced a shortage of heating fuel, we thought that having abundant supplies of coal for heating would be an asset for some far-sighted people. But it did not work out this way. After the house had been on the market one year, we had the coal furnace torn out, and a new high-efficiency gas furnace installed. We lived in the house the next winter with the new gas furnace, and at times, we felt like we would freeze to death with the different heating system. The coal furnace had given us good, even heat, whereas the gas furnace would allow the house to become cold during intervals when it would trip off and shut down, before it would turn on and produce heat again! Finally, in the spring of 1991, the house was sold, and we could proceed with plans to move to our newly remodeled home on Ponto Lake. There we had installed both a wood and gas furnace, and during cold weather, we could use the wood heat to provide even heat once again. It might be added that we were among the last residences in Superior to use coal heat, and it was probably only a short time before coal would not be available from suppliers for single residences!

Packing up belongings in our Superior home and garage was quite a task. We threw away many items, took clothes to the Goodwill Store, and gave away a variety of items, and yet had many boxes of goods to pack in the U-Haul truck I rented. Being pack rats, especially me, was now something we were paying for in the form of hard work. Lee and his family helped us load the truck. We rented the largest size U-Haul truck available, and when we filled it, we still had much left over. We also owned a small pick-up truck, and we had been using it to move small furniture and other boxes of goods and take these over to Ponto every time we made a trip there. We left some items in the garage, such as a new window awning that I wish we had taken time to move to Ponto. Finally, we placed the last movable object in the truck, and we took off for our Ponto home. Mollee rode with me in the truck while Barbara drove our car. Sue, Becky, and other family members were waiting for us to help unload when we arrived at Ponto. I had hoped to avert filling the trailer home, which was my study, with overflow items. But as the house and garage filled up, we had to place more and more possessions in the trailer home. Finally, everything was unloaded, and after what had seemed like a long time, all our worldly possessions were in one location! Glory be! However, there were many days ahead of absorbing all we had brought over into our already rather full dwellings! It would appear we were far more materialistic minded than I had realized. I wished, as Barbara had warned, that we had put the brakes on our buying habits. Certainly, I was the main culprit here for Barbara was much more restrained in her consumption than I was. Barbara rather frequently pointed out in conversations that I could not turn down a good bargain. Put a clearance tag on some merchandise and I had great difficulty in passing it by!

Earlier in August 1988, the children had a reception/party for my retirement and our fortieth wedding anniversary. Forty years of marriage had rushed by, and it was difficult to believe this was happening. What an adventurous forty years this had been. And we hoped it was far from over. We looked forward to exciting new experiences ahead. And our revitalized home at Ponto provided a perfect base to launch these new adventures. Consequently, since this prior reception/party had been held, there was no overt celebration of our finally getting moved. There should have been! It had developed into a major family undertaking.

A few years earlier, Becky had remarried. A cousin had introduced her to a young man in the Twin Cities, and they soon began dating. As they became better acquainted, they wished to marry and were married in Texas where Denny, her fiancé, was employed. Sue and her cousin, Diana flew down for the wedding. Somewhat later, Becky came to us and inquired if we would be willing to sell them some of our lake property for they would like to have a place on Ponto. We discussed this and agreed to let them have two hundred feet of lakeshore between our home and the Gardner home. The lot was grown over

DEEPLY FLOW THE LOVE CURRENTS

with dense brush, and we had some humorous moments getting lost as we worked on clearing the lot. The year-around home was finished by about the time that I retired, and my retirement observance and our fortieth anniversary celebration were held back on the grounds of their new home. How great it was to have them near us. This development could really be included among the new adventures shaping up for the future!

Now that we were settled at Ponto, we wished to go South for part of the coming winter. We found out that renting a condo was not easy with us taking our dog with us. So we began to consider purchasing a travel trailer and pick-up truck to drive down South. Our good friends, Dick and Dorothy Walters, planned to meet us in Florida for they were already "R.V. people." So we began looking around for a trailer and truck.

We found a used travel trailer owned by a couple in a neighboring town, and we purchased a pick-up truck at a local car dealer. On the way down to Florida, we stopped the first night and stayed with good friends of long standing in Pekin, Illinois, and the second night we stayed at a small R.V. park in northeastern Missouri. This park had rather primitive accommodations. We thought this was probably typical of R. V. parks, and we were not very enthusiastic about relegating ourselves to parks like this in our future adventures in "RVing." As it turned out, this park was one of the least desirable ones we ever stayed in.

Dick and Dorothy were waiting for us at a park near Ft. Walton Beach, Florida. This park was right on a sound off the Gulf. We spent about a week camping with the Walters, and this proved to be one of the more enjoyable times we experienced in our R. V. trips to the South. We were off to a good start in our camping experiences. But this was not the whole story.

On our drive back home, we encountered snow and strong winds in central Illinois. A few miles north of Bloomington, Illinois, we suddenly hit a slick stretch of highway and the truck began to go in one direction, and the trailer in another direction. Oncoming cars on the two—lane highway were approaching, and it appeared that we were going to have a bad accident. Barbara remembered our recent reading of information on driving with travel trailers and how the booklet read to apply gradually the trailer brake lever, which was just under the dashboard of the truck between us, and this would bring the "rig" out of such a spin. Calmly, she did this, and our truck and trailer straightened out just before we met the oncoming traffic. Barbara was the heroine of the morning! This incident, however, rather put a damper on us pulling the trailer south for the next couple of winters, and it remained parked out in the yard at our Ponto home.

This was not to last, though, for we purchased a new travel trailer about two years later and thus renewed our trips south to break up the winter months. Altogether, we made over a dozen trips south with different travel trailers. We loved these trips to the South, and after the first trip with its near accident, we made them with few complications. Some of our friends wondered why in the world we wanted to be bothered with all the preparations and potentials for danger in traveling this way. Barbara's pet answer to this question nearly always was, "This way, we have our own beds and our own dirt!" And so it was!

My cousin, Darrell, and his wife, Betty, lived in the Pensacola metropolitan area, and their hospitality and assistance definitely contributed to our camping enjoyment in the area. Sometimes we stayed in a trailer park not far from their home, and many nights we played various card games with them. In central Florida, in the course of several years, we stayed in the same small park and became acquainted with a number of the families. We even discovered that a fraternity brother of mine had a winter home only a few miles from this park, and we had some memorable fellowship with them. Anita Adams lived close by in Winter Haven, and we often ate at restaurants with her and visited frequently with her in her home. She and her late husband were the couple we had frequently been with back at Drake when Barbara and I were dating. In fact, as mentioned earlier, her husband, Court, and I were in fourth grade together, back in Ft. Madison, Iowa. Family and friends like these added much to the richness of the experiences we enjoyed in our camping days in Florida.

Then there were the two times we went to Texas and New Mexico for a change. Again, we were fortunate to be with friends. Darrell's older brother, Wayne, and his wife, lived in Las Cruces, New Mexico, and we camped near there for two weeks and very much enjoyed being with them. Our good friends, John and Wilma Snyder from Decatur, Illinois, went every winter to R.V. camps near Mission, Texas. We camped next to them for two weeks and had fellowship that only choice superlatives could begin to describe. An extra bonus there were the musical jam sessions where John often was MC. These were held in the recreation halls of various parks and were usually supported by large audiences. Then there were the two weeks we occupied the adjacent site to Louie and Velma Brockhagen, (our neighbors back at Ponto), in a park near Fredericksburg, Texas. This, too, was a time of much appreciated company. Not only did we enjoy breaking up the long Minnesota winters, but being with old and new friends "added icing to the cake!" We frequently said that the people in these parks were friendly, down-to-earth individuals, but also folks who respected each other's privacy. Also, we could park our modest travel trailers next to motor homes costing in the hundreds of thousands of dollars and find that there were really no status differences displayed. A welcome relief from the stratification that often existed on college campuses!

Clouds Appear on the Horizon

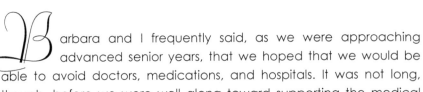

arbara and I frequently said, as we were approaching advanced senior years, that we hoped that we would be able to avoid doctors, medications, and hospitals. It was not long, though, before we were well along toward supporting the medical industry. Our kitchen counter began to look like a small pharmacy. Trips to various physicians became almost routine, and even hospitals were not avoided! Our days of being relatively free from these medical resources were rapidly ending.

At age eighty-three, Barbara was informed by a cardiologist at Abbot Northwestern in Minneapolis that she needed a heart bypass. I well recall when Becky and I were in the room and when the cardiologist told us this that I exclaimed, "Oh, I didn't want to hear that!" The next day, she had this surgery. One humorous incident happened while she was not fully recovered from the anesthesia. Just she and I were in her hospital room, and she remarked as she was musing, "You know I am no spring chicken anymore!" Then she looked over at me and declared, "You're not either!" No longer could we bask in the "myths" that we were spring chickens!

Although she did have some repercussions after she was discharged from Abbot Northwestern, for an octogenarian, Barbara did rather remarkably come back from this surgery. The surgery did contribute, though, to her walking somewhat bent over and she gradually developed a rather pronounced case of osteoporosis. At times, she suffered from rather severe back pain. Several times, she was treated by a physical therapist and physicians for this problem.

In the meantime, I had noticed some shortness of breath, and tests revealed that I needed some stints to relieve some blocked heart arteries. So a couple of years after Barbara's heart bypass surgery, I had five stints inserted at Abbot Northwestern. Other health problems began to create their respective discomforts and annoyances, and more and more, we realized that age was beginning to leave its marks upon us. Grey clouds were commencing to appear on the horizon.

Nevertheless, compared with many of our peers, we realized that we were fortunate to have as good health as we experienced. Another sobering situation was emerging, namely that we were aware that we were outliving many of our friends. Our ranks were thinning, and this contributed to certain loneliness that advancing age can readily bring about. Age—show you not any mercy?!

But we cannot saddle these years as sad, melancholy, and unpleasant years. On more than one occasion, Barbara exclaimed that these recent years had been the best years of our marriage. And in many ways, they were. A conscious closeness, a special kind of rapport, and deepening love was occurring that more than offset the approaching, unwelcome clouds on the horizon. The last few years of our comradeship and ties were strengthening in ways far beyond any expectations or prior preparation. Advancing age does have its positive secrets!

Of course, our family and close friends provided love and support that under girded much of this inner peace and security. Our children respected and honored the decisions we made, but were always available to help us when needed. We knew we could depend upon them. Our ties with the Brainerd Friends Meeting (Quakers) and the Northwoods Unitarian/Universalist Fellowship were strong and much appreciated. At times, they brought in food and kept in frequent touch with us to see how we were.

As Barbara grew weaker and less and less able to do various tasks for herself, I assumed more and more responsibilities for her care. I felt it was a privilege and even an honor to care for her. I had been doing most of the cooking for some time. Barbara said I was a good cook, but I laughed and stated that she declared this for she felt she had no other options to my cooking. For the most part, I made my cooking as simple as possible, although occasionally I would branch out and prepare a more elaborate meal. We both were thankful to be together, and quite frequently Barbara would say, "I'm so glad we are still together!" Our gratefulness for being together grew moment by moment. Love diminished the difficulties that were confronting us, and I really experienced at a minimum the demands placed upon me. Our children and friends from time to time would say, "Noel, you have to be careful or you are going to wear yourself out, and then you won't be any good to anyone!" I heard them, but at the same time, I pretty much ignored their well—intended cautionary remarks.

In February 2011, we sat down to eat our breakfast. No noticeable change had been observed in Barbara's health in recent days, and then suddenly, she just was unable to do anything for herself. She just sat at the breakfast table with her head down and saying or doing nothing. Becky stopped by about then, and I gestured to her that I did not know what had just happened. We helped her back to the couch, and she just lay there uncommunicative. With such near complete helplessness on her part, I knew the point had been reached where I could not continue to care for her by myself. We had to do something.

Reluctantly, we phoned our physician and told him what was happening. We indicated that we feared the time had arrived when we had to think about placing Barbara in a nursing facility. Our doctor recommended we bring her down to the emergency room at the Brainerd Hospital and have her evaluated. So we prepared to drive Barbara to the hospital. (In recent weeks, we had taken her to the ER at the hospital several times.) After checking her, the physician at the ER called Becky, Denny, and me outside the room she was in and said that Barbara appeared to be in the dying process. I strongly stated that I was not ready to give up, so she was admitted to stay in the hospital overnight while her situation was further evaluated.

The next morning, a social worker came in to Barbara's hospital room and announced that arrangements had been made to move Barbara to a skilled nursing facility in Walker. I responded saying, "Oh, I don't want to move her to Walker, but to Walker she was moved. Barbara rode with Becky in her car since it rode more smoothly than our car. I followed with our car. Becky said the drive to Walker was a most memorable ride, and Barbara was awake and alert most of the trip. I hated to think what was going on, for I had hoped that placing Barbara in a nursing facility would never have to happen. But I realized that this was probably the only realistic option open to us. My hope had not been abandoned, and I continued to hope that Barbara could be nursed back to health and leave the facility in Walker and return home.

We were in the room where Barbara would stay, and we were discussing with the staff whether to enter in her admittance records if we wanted her to have resuscitation. I was having some difficulty in making a decision on this matter. We did not realize that Barbara was listening to and following this discussion, when all at once in a loud, assertive voice she declared, "When I die, I want to die!" The answer had been given by Barbara concerning the issue of resuscitation!

Barbara had a roommate that we all came to love and trust. She was recovering from foot surgery, and she and Barbara had excellent rapport from the very beginning. She kept an eye on Barbara, and if Barbara needed assistance, she would see that Barbara received such. Actually, Barbara had understanding, competent, and compassionate care at the Walker home, and we never had any major complaints. For the first part of her stay in the home, she seemed to display improvement in her health. Physical therapy commenced early, and we were somewhat optimistic about the care she was receiving. Her prognosis was encouraging. The three weeks she was there, I only missed a couple of days, driving the forty-five—minute drive from our home to Walker. On the days I did not make the drive, Becky was there to be with her. Often I fed Barbara her main meal, and she ate well the first several days; but then she began to eat less and less. We became increasingly concerned if she was going to recover.

On March 19th, at the recommendation of the staff at Walker, Barbara was taken to the hospital in Park Rapids for medical evaluation. Sue came that weekend, and we drove up to Park Rapids on the twentieth to see Barbara. Never will I forget seeing Barbara alone in her hospital room at Park Rapids, and she looked so lonely and isolated. I would have liked to gone over to her bed and picked her up and hugged her! The situation tore into me. The doctor at the hospital and nurse who had been attending Barbara, said there was nothing more they could do for her there, and they were ready to dismiss her and have her return to the nursing facility in Walker. A medical van drove her back to Walker, and we drove ahead to the Walker home. After she was resettled in her bed at Walker, we stayed with her awhile. Our granddaughter, Nikkee, had now joined us, and the three of us, after a rather brief visit, kissed her and returned back to our Ponto home. Yes, I regret that I did not stay with Barbara that evening. She was more or less unresponsive to us, although she knew who we were. Again, she looked so much by herself when we left her in her room that Sunday afternoon.

The next morning, the three of us were preparing to drive back to Walker to see Barbara. Sue and Nikkee were out taking a walk when our phone rang, and it was the nurse at Walker telling me that they were cleaning up Barbara when she just stopped breathing. Barbara had died. I said we were coming up there and would soon be there. Of course, I cried out when I heard this news, and I went out and called to Sue and Nikkee, and the three of us hugged and cried together. I had feared for some time that her death was approaching, but I was a long way from being willing to give her up. A vital part of me and our family life had been subtracted. Death—, a universal occurrence, yet a very private experience—had taken place, and life would never be the same again!

In a rather selfish way, I had hoped that I would be the first to depart this life. Barbara, I felt, would be able to adjust much better than I to our separation. In what is referred to as presocialization, I had tried to prepare for life without Barbara, but such an effort had been quite inadequate. It was almost impossible for me to imagine not having Barbara around. She was so much a part of my life. Few were the activities in which we engaged without the other one. Sometimes when I was planning to drive into town to run a few errands and she had decided to stay at home, at the last minute, she would say, "Wait a moment. I think I shall go with you after all," and I would wait for her to slip on her coat or jacket and go with me. In the car, it was always so reassuring to look over and see her sitting there beside me in the passenger seat. (She did not drive the last few years of her life.) Togetherness was the enduring theme of our married life. Togetherness in our privacy, togetherness in our social life, togetherness in our intellectual pursuits, togetherness in our spiritual growth.

Now the presocialization that I had awkwardly attempted to practice was to be put into action. The reality of togetherness broken, directly confronted me. Barbara, I did not want this. Whoever had been the pilot and copilot now had no copilot! Aloneness, absent your omnipresent support, missing your magic touch—. These now dominated the picture. Tears cannot restore the past. Fond memories? Yes. But they cannot fill the vacuum. Yes, life can never be the same again!

Noel and Barbara
2006
Celebrating fifty years at their home
on Ponto lake

PART V

Life Is, Indeed, Adventurous

Who says marriage is dull?
Yes, it can be among the greatest adventures one can experience!

Contributing Factors to
This Love Story

umerous comments were made by others about our marriage. Never will I forget a few months before Barbara's death, one of our granddaughters came down to my study when I was working alone at my desk and said, "Grandpa, I just wanted to tell you how your marriage with Grandma has been a great inspiration to me. You are a mentor to me in your marriage!" A young lady who graciously helped us from time to time with cleaning the main floor of our home and had had numerous opportunities to observe Barbara's and my relationship on several occasions remarked that the two of us were passionately in love with one another. A nurse at the Walker nursing facility commented once to me, "You two are like two peas in a pod!" as she referred to her observations of our ties with one another.

And so the observations and comments were articulated by others. Yes, indeed, our marriage was a close one. It came close to being a total relationship as some writers in the field of marriage classify our kind of marital ties. Our lives were close to being totally enmeshed with one another. Our feelings, our thoughts, our interests, our values, our perspectives, etc., were close to being indistinguishable from one another. While this was not exactly true in our courtship days and early on in our marriage, as the years passed, they became more like this as our common, shared interests and activities grew together.

No doubt there would be those critics who would say such totality was not healthy and that our marriage did not leave enough room for the expression of our individuality. Some of the more harsh critics would probably go so far as to say that we "smothered" one another! We were not "liberated" individuals. Our lives were dominated by our togetherness and extreme blending, they would declare. But one cannot help but wonder if such critics have ever, themselves, tasted the joys, the mutual confidence, the trust, the extensive sharing of almost the total range of their lives, as we did? Are such critics perhaps saturated with the American culture's emphasis upon individuality and the priorities demanded by such an emphasis? Yes, I feel no need for any apology for the overwhelming love that Barbara and I experienced. If our marriage was an exceptional one—good! Thankful, I am, indeed, that our marriage did not possess the thin veneer of a marital status covering two unhappy and anxious individuals preoccupied with their individualities.

What contributed to the kind of love and marriage that Barbara and I experienced? Many conditions and factors that were present in our lives and our relationship could be mentioned, but only a few can be set forth here. These are among the characteristics that I believe helped to strengthen and enter into making our marriage a rather exceptional one:

First, we soon developed a mutual trust. We were confident in each one being open and honest with the other. Concealment of important matters was absent in our relationship. Easy, relaxed comfort with one another was an early development in our relationship.

Second, we stayed out of debt for the most part. Only some of the first cars we purchased and later mortgages on our homes can be cited as debts we incurred, and these did not last very long. Except for gas cards, we scarcely knew what credit cards were in our early marriage. Later when we did possess credit cards, we used them sparingly and usually only when we were traveling. Fortunate we were that we never did have to worry about the pressures of extensive debts.

Third, we avoided playing the "status game." Campus life among faculty members was conducive to being a part of this game, but if we played it at all, it was a bare minimum. Conspicuous consumption was almost totally absent in our lives. Advertising ploys failed with us. We lived comfortably, but not extravagantly.

Fourth, sex was important, of course, but it did not dominate our lives. It did not crowd out numerous other pleasures and enjoyable pursuits in our routine living. One might almost refer to sex as an extra bonus that married life provided, not as the essence of our marriage!

Fifth, we had common religious backgrounds. There were not large gaps in our mutual beliefs nor practices. As our religious views changed through the years, we discussed them and were aware that they were similar and supportive for each of us. Once in the church we were attending, the minister declared in his sermon ideas that were offensive to us and only after the service did we mention to one another that independently, we each considered about getting up and walking out of the service! Our views were open to each of us and were supportive rather than antagonistic or threatening.

Sixth, we respected and supported each other on how the children were raised. Seldom, if ever, did either one of us attempt to interfere with how the other one was disciplining, treating, or relating to any of our children. Barbara was better at talking with our daughters and engaging in personal, confidential conversation with them, than I was. I must admit that, at times, I was slightly envious of how easily Barbara related to our daughters. Lee and I had rather good rapport, but not as thorough as Barbara did with Becky and Sue. Our relationship with Philip was more varied. He was six years old when he came to be a part of our family and had already established patterns and habits of interaction with his foster home parents. But any conflict with one another over our relationships with our children was absent from the scene.

Seventh, while we likely paid a price for our avoidance of the use of intoxicating beverages in the way of suffering through, unaided by the relief of such beverages for our pains, stress, and anxieties, and some social ostracism from others, we continued the influences of our parental homes where intoxicating drinks were never consumed nor served. By so doing, our lives were not complicated by the risks of such consumption, especially heavy consumption, leading to mild or serious forms of alcoholism. Other tendencies of superficial feelings of well—being were also discouraged from developing by our abstinence.* I was about a 95 percent teetotaler, and Barbara was about a 99 percent one! We belonged to a vanishing "breed" of Americans. **

Eighth, with few exceptions, our close ties with other couples were with individuals who had strong marriages. Divorce or talk of divorce was missing in our friendships. Our social life was among other couples who shared many of the same marital and family values as we did.

Ninth, we shared many common interests. We liked simple amusements and entertainment. Window shopping on our trips would be an example of an activity that probably numerous individuals would consider boring, but we enjoyed strolling along together doing this. Until her hearing problems developed, we liked listening to classic and semi classic records and cassettes. We found playing card games with one another a very pleasant recreational pursuit. We liked working together in the garden. Picnics were a favorite outing—and on and on, one could go citing common interests we shared.

Tenth, humor, teasing one another, light-hearted conversation, and antics were refreshingly common in our being together. This was a healthy antidote to taking each other or events too seriously. But this requires a section of its own.

*Sometimes I would consider modifying my behavior regarding my occasional use of intoxicating beverages, and then I would have students stop by and relate to me the problems alcohol was causing in their families, and I would veto modifying my behavior.

** In connection with our behavior regarding the use of intoxicating beverages, an amusing incident happened at Sue and Craig's wedding rehearsal dinner. Craig's parents knew of our near—teetotaler behavior, and they were somewhat ill at ease in how we might react to the serving of wine at the dinner. Our granddaughter, Mollee, who was just a youngster, was sitting at the same table with us. Somehow, I accidentally spilled my wine glass as we were sitting at the table, and Mollee yelled out in a voice that could be heard all over the large dining room, "Grandpa spilled his wine! Grandpa spilled his wine!" That was one of the few times I could have choked my granddaughter!

Good, Old Humor

*A*mong my numerous faults is teasing and kidding individuals which at times I overdo. This behavior has probably been intensified by my sociological training. Writers have asserted that "debunking" is a characteristic of sociological study and practice, and I fear I acquired a generous dose of this in becoming a sociologist. I must confess that I have enjoyed deflating the egos of pompous, self-appointed intellectuals who pride themselves with their superior knowledge and understanding. Debunking is a helpful tool in reducing overly serious thought and activity. While often I was not aware of debunking, Barbara sensed its presence, I am sure, when we were among other people.

It took Barbara awhile to become used to my teasing and injection of humor into our lives. Her father had teased her at times, and it was not that she was totally unaccustomed to it, but with me I guess, one could say it was a very common part of my behavior. Once she adjusted to it, she played the game admirably, making light of much of what we said and did. Barbara was fun to be with. She was very good company. After all, she was my life companion. A number of examples can be cited of fun times together.

One of the favorite stories I have cited numerous times was our driving out of the lane back to our Ponto home. On the last curve, as one left our place, were some trees close to the road. It had been slick, and I had come close to sliding in to one of the trees on the curve. One of the next times we were driving out to the highway, Barbara cautioned to watch that tree. I drove a short distance on and stopped the car just before we reached the curve and stopped. After a few minutes had passed, Barbara declared, "Noel, what are you doing?" I replied, "I'm watching the tree!" We had to laugh about this incident.

We were driving back from Pine River to our Ponto home at dusk one fall evening and Barbara had been talking with little let up in her part of the conversation. Teasingly, I said that she was doing a lot of unusual talking, and she replied, "O.K., I won't say another word until we get home." A few seconds later, it seemed that a deer without warning almost dropped out of the sky in front of the car, and I hit it head—on. We both yelled, and she excitedly said something about the collision. Recovering from the shock, I stated, "Boy, you ended your silence all of a sudden!" Again, we laughed at the brief silence of talking that had occurred.

In the unplanned division of tasks around the house, Barbara had taken on the job of replacing the toilet soap at the lavatory when it was needed. Usually, she allowed the soap to get down to just a sliver before replacing it. One day, I rigged up a magnifying glass and placed it over the sliver of soap. It was not long before she saw what had been done, and I forget what she said, but she had a forceful and appropriate retort.

On one of our trips with the travel trailer, it was approaching the late afternoon, and we had stopped at a trailer park for the night. After we had been inside the trailer for a short time, Barbara said, "Boy, those trailer lights don't seem to be giving out much light." I looked at her and said, "Dear, you still have your sunglasses on!" We both enjoyed this amusing incident.

On one return trip from Central Florida, we were driving west along the highway out of Perry, Florida, when Barbara announced that she was beginning to need a restroom rather badly. This stretch of highway was a very isolated area with service stations almost absent from the scene. On both sides of the road were large drainage ditches that looked like they could be crawling with alligators and poisonous snakes. Any emergency stop there appeared out of the question. Barbara's plight was worsening by the minute, and we did not know what we were going to do. Then suddenly, I exclaimed, "Idiots, idiots. What are we pulling behind us?" Behind us, of course, was our modern travel trailer with a convenient bathroom. As soon as her predicament was eased, we both had a big laugh about this occurrence.

One of Barbara's favorite stories related to when we were living in Albion. This was relatively early in our marriage, and once in the mood of a young, vain groom, I had mentioned to Barbara that it would be nice when I came home from the campus for lunch, if she would be more attractively dressed. Soon after this, Barbara went to great lengths to dress in a hilarious manner. She wore an old housedress, blacked out one of her teeth, put on old stockings that drooped down around her shoes, messed up her hair, etc. I had had a rather difficult morning at school, and I came in the door and never so much as noticed how she was dressed! This comical moment was told more elaborately every time Barbara related it. So much for my powers of observation! Barbara apparently was correct when she often declared that I was not very observing!

Frequently, I arose earlier in the morning than Barbara. When she was getting up, she often came to the bedroom door and would slowly bend down lower and lower while I did the same out in whatever part of the house I happened to be. This, I guess, we did to give the appearance that we wanted to make sure that she was finally up and preparing for the new day. Also, when she was later than usual in arising, I would say when she appeared, "Good afternoon." Just silly fun!

We were both raised as only children. Rather often when one of us displayed a rather self-centered kind of behavior, we would say to the other one, "Your only child complex is showing!" This would bring forth grins on our parts.

On our frequent walks together down our lane, Barbara would pick up or kick sticks aside that had fallen during the night. Often, these were not very large sticks. I would then stoop over and pick up twigs that almost required a magnifying glass to see. Her response often would be, "Oh, stop it!"

After our children and family seldom stayed in the cottage and house with us at Ponto, Barbara acquired that extra bedroom and hung her clothes in the closet of this room. In fact, this room came to be considered her room. The closet I used for my clothes was packed and usually running over with them. She had extra room in her closet, and every so often, I would parade in front of her with an arm full of clothes and pretend that I was going to hang them in her closet. "Oh, no you don't," she would exclaim, and there would be a brief, supposedly serious, conversation about the situation. Of course, I never won!

Sometimes our behavior was nothing but slapstick antics. While we lived in North Carolina, we made a trip to Florida with Barbara's parents. A seaside cottage was rented for a couple of nights near Daytona Beach. We were excited to have been able to rent a beach cottage, so after we were settled in, Barbara's Dad and I dressed up in gaudy clothes and did an improvised dance in the dwelling while Barbara and her mother joined in. On another occasion, our good friend, Idris, was visiting us, and I announced that we would have church services out on our deck. I dressed up in an outlandish bright bathrobe, draped a scarf around my neck and placed a furry, splashy cap on my head, and went out, and sat down in the glider on our deck and waited for the women to appear. Soon through the door came Idris and Barbara dressed in high heels, unusual dresses, and broad—brimmed hats. If anyone passed by and saw us, they would have thought a group of mental patients had escaped! Such antics broke up any solemnity that might have been developing for the morning!

This is only a good start of times we enjoyed our spontaneous humor, teasing, and antics. If an observer were limited to these occasions in what he knew about us, he/she would think we never had a serious thought in our lives. But for us, they rounded out our marriage and lives in a manner that embellished the fun and pleasures of being together.

Concluding Thoughts

Much do I regret that this love story was not written while Barbara was still alive. It needed her input. I hope that I have not grossly misrepresented the realities of what is written here. I am sure she would have added incidents and perspectives that I have neglected. The idea for this book and some of the initial stories were roughly jotted down before her death. It is my fault that it was not composed while Barbara was living, and at least the story could have benefited from her critical eye to this draft. Few of my writings were ever written without her first reading the draft and making valuable suggestions.

Recently, I told some friends that I possess a serious disease. It is called "inertia," and it is chronic. I have had this difficulty for a long time, and it can be blamed, to some extent, for the delay in writing this love story.

Writing this story has brought back many memories. Only a few could be included in this transcript. Oh, how I loved Barbara, and I believe the feeling was mutual. We were "soul mates" strongly implying that we were more than just a conventional married couple. Barbara provided a sense of well—being that was impossible to find with anyone else. While I am extremely thankful for our family and good friends and their gracious support, there is a vital part of my life that is missing. There is now an incompleteness present that for the sixty-two years of our marriage did not exist.

Yes, I do believe in some kind of immortality. Supposedly, being highly educated with a Ph.D. from a prestigious university, some of my colleagues would likely assert that Noel never quite matured. He continues to believe in a divinity and immortality. If this is immaturity, so let them believe it. I cannot accept the fact that a loving; understanding, and compassionate Creator would make it possible for us humans to experience the kind of love that Barbara and I shared, and then at what we call death, have it suddenly evaporate into nothing! I believe in some way that surpasses our imagination and grasp that our loved ones are not gone forever. This I was believing and struggling with some time before Barbara died. But enough of this thought for now. I am just declaring my conviction here. I am not trying to convince anyone.

Hopefully, sharing this love story with others can contribute to their own awareness of the amazing wonders that our human lives can bring to us. Many characteristics can block the fulfillment of these wonders in our lives—fear, reluctance to live more open lives, unhealthy egotisms, misdirected pride, etc. Perhaps those writers are correct who emphasize that the culprit in our lives that prevent really living and sharing abundant living is the fear of not being loved. Most likely, early in my life, I was burdened with this malady, but Barbara, you pulverized it!

Thankful That . . .

Barbara—

I am thankful that you provided the opportunity for me to spend over sixty-two years with you as your husband, companion, friend, and soul mate.-

I am thankful that you never helped engender or fuel any really serious arguments or disagreements.-

I am thankful that you never held grudges.-

I am thankful that you avoided nagging, nor, in some unconscious manner, encouraged me to nag.-

I am thankful that you were open and flexible in your thinking and yet had underlying values that guided you and your family.-

I am thankful that you were receptive to living in new environments and meeting new challenges.-

I am thankful that you excelled in providing stability and serenity for me and our family.-

I am thankful that you were never too busy or too preoccupied to listen to me and our children.-

I am thankful that you were a more careful and restrained consumer of goods than I.-

I am thankful that you could find much to love and cherish in simple and unpretentious living.-

I am thankful that gossip was almost foreign to your lips.-

I am thankful for the easy, natural, and contagious way you could provide the needed kind of support and empathy in times of trouble for me and our family.-

I am thankful that you soon learned to accept and receive kidding and making fun of what could have been overly serious moments in our lives—even when it appeared to be carried a little bit to the extreme.-

I am thankful that you did not carry your feelings around on your sleeves.-

I am thankful that being a person of integrity just came naturally with you.-

I am thankful that you avoided putting me on a pedestal—that you accepted me as I am.-

I am thankful for your being just you, not afraid to be yourself in all situations nor trying to camouflage who you really were.-

How blessed was I to know and love you! HOW BLESSED TO KNOW AND LOVE YOU!

APPENDIX

Unlike appendixes often are, what is included here is no less important, as far as I am concerned, than what has already been written.

Our Sixty-Third Wedding Anniversary

08/18/11

Deeply Flow the Love Currents

Today would have been our sixty-third wedding anniversary
Of course I wish you were here to help celebrate
And of course I do miss you very much.
The months seem more like years since your death.

Countless memories have been recalled these months
And today they have especially been forthcoming
That garden wedding and tea room luncheon
And the trip north with you riding by my side.

How much more meaningful would they be if
You were here to recall these memories with me
For reminiscing together always tuned the memories
To a special and colorful pleasure.

Where have these sixty-three years gone, dear?
Is it really true that it has been this long?
Time plays tricks upon us, doesn't it?
Long ago, the wedding occurred, yet it was only yesterday!

How thankful I am for the wondrous marriage we shared
Truly it was as near perfect as a marriage can be
You will always be my bride—my sweetheart-
Enduring, inspiring will you ever continue to be!

Handwritten Notes from Barbara

(By this time, it was rather difficult for Barbara to write.)

To Noel

On Christmas 2008: To tell you that I love you very much!
You are the greatest companion anyone could have. We have great
fun together!

I would rather be with you than anyone else!! Thank you for sharing your
life with me.

Barbara

Father's Day: (June 2010)

Dear Noel

This being Father's Day, I want to tell you how much I love you. It grows
more with each day.

Our time together has been and is being so wonderful.

I love you!!!
Barbara

Appendix
Clarification

Many more incidents and events in our married life could be added here, but I have attempted to avoid making this love story too tedious and prolonged. However, since this writing states that our seven vibrant granddaughters are among those to whom the book is dedicated, more mention should be made about our valued relationships with them. Our latest great—granddaughter, Lucy, was born after Barbara's death, so Barbara missed seeing this cheerful, good—natured baby. Certainly, this is to be regretted. The other great—granddaughter, Rena, Barbara did see. She got to hold her and sense what a lively, precocious child was developing.

Mollee and Nikkee, Lee's daughters, we were around more often as they were growing up than the others, and this was due to the fact that their parents were both working, and Barbara shared with their other grandmother, June, taking care of them when they were toddlers and youngsters while their parents were at work. We had the wonderful experience, then, of sharing in this raising of two inquisitive, delightful granddaughters. Many amusing and memorable experiences could be cited here. An example would be one day at lunch time, I said we would bow our heads and observe our grace in silence. When we raised our heads from grace, Nikkee (about three years old then) exclaimed, "What was that all about?"

Sue's daughters, Emily and Jackie, we were not around as often when they were young. They lived near International Falls, some distance from us, and we only were with them when they came to visit us with their parents or on the limited occasions when we went to visit them. We have a prized video of them as preschool children holding hands and singing how they harmoniously got along together because they were sisters (although it was not always this way!!).

Marcia, Becky's daughter and our youngest granddaughter, grew up in the Metro area, and again, we missed being around her during those crucial developmental years. However, when she was about twelve, her parents moved to their lake home next to us, and we were then able to see her more often. When Barbara was having sight problems, she used to come over to our place and help her grandmother with her reading.

Certainly, these granddaughters added inestimable joy and satisfaction to our lives. As an old saying goes, we could enjoy them, but seldom did we have the responsibility for their care twenty-four hours a day! Our earlier energies and caring abilities had seemed to decrease with age as we came into the grandparent stage of our lives! Long ago, such as in their computer and electronic skills and knowledge, have they left us way behind. It has been a challenge and a struggle avoiding falling too far behind them. And even though at various times they have ganged up on their grandfather, it is great to be a grandparent. IT IS GREAT TO BE A GRANDPARENT!